She Went to the Field

WOMEN SOLDIERS OF THE CIVIL WAR

She Went to the Field

Women Soldiers of the Civil War

Bonnie Tsui

TWODOT®

GUILFORD, CONNECTICUT
HELENA, MONTANA
AN IMPRINT OF THE GLOBE PEQUOT PRESS

A · TWODOT® · BOOK

Copyright © 2003 by Bonnie Tsui

All rights reserved. No part of this book may be reproduced or transmitted in any form by any means, electronic or mechanical, including photocopying and recording, or by any information storage and retrieval system, except as may be expressly permitted by the 1976 Copyright Act or by the publisher. Requests for permission should be made in writing to The Globe Pequot Press, P.O. Box 480, Guilford, Connecticut 06437.

TwoDot is a registered trademark of The Globe Pequot Press.

Text design by Lisa Reneson

Library of Congress Cataloging-in-Publication Data is available.

ISBN 0-7627-2438-2

Manufactured in the United States of America
First Edition/First Printing

Dedication

I dedicate this book to my family, especially my mother, Selena, for always being there. And to my love, Matthew—thanks for making me laugh throughout.

Contents

Acknowledgments

THE IDEA FOR THIS COLLECTION of profiles was conceived when I was a teenager. In the school library, I came across a dusty old book about a girl who dressed as a boy to fight in the American Civil War. The story inspired me to write a fanciful historical novella of my own on the subject, and the interest never left me. It developed further in a research paper I wrote for a class with Civil War historian William Gienapp at Harvard University, and my exploration was kindly encouraged by teaching fellow Libra Hilde. Why had the achievement of these women soldiers not yet seized the popular imagination? I am grateful that the project has at last come to fruition with my editor, Charlene Patterson, and the history imprint at The Globe Pequot Press.

More thanks to: Colonel Herbert E. Halliday, for his stories, his expertise in military history, and for connecting me to an invaluable resource, the U.S. Army Military History Institute; Sarah Hutcheon at the Arthur and Elizabeth Schlesinger Library on the History of Women in America, Radcliffe Institute for Advanced Study, Harvard University; Leslie Fields, Associate Curator at the Gilder Lehrman Collection of the Pierpont Morgan Library; Laurel Ulrich; James Duncan Philips, Professor of Early American History and Director of the Charles Warren Center for Studies in American History, Harvard University; Drew Faust, Professor of History and Dean of the Radcliffe Institute for

Advanced Study, Harvard University; Laura Pappano, my original mentor and guide; and Marsha Osrow and Michael Dolber, who set me on this path so long ago.

Introduction

"Lots of boys enlisted under the wrong name. So did I. The country needed men, and I wanted excitement."

—Albert D. J. Cashier, Co. G,
Ninety-fifth Illinois Infantry, aka Jennie Hodgers

DURING THE AMERICAN CIVIL WAR, 1861–1865, women from the North and South disguised themselves as men and enlisted in their respective armies. In the late 1880s, when Civil War nurse and soldiers' aid activist Mary Livermore heard the speculation that at least 400 women "bore arms and served in the ranks" for the Union army, she wrote in her autobiography that though she couldn't "vouch for the correctness of this estimate," she was "convinced that a larger number of women disguised themselves and enlisted in the service, for one cause or other, than was dreamed of."

Scholars today estimate that about 250 women joined the Southern troops and that up to 1,000 women may have enlisted in both the Confederate and Union armies. These women warriors represent an enduring historical trend of women posing as men to fight patriotically in battle, both in fact and popular fiction—from twelfth-century French (and later English) queen Eleanor of Aquitaine to Joan of Arc to the American Revolutionary War's Deborah Sampson to fictional heroine

1

Sarah Brewer in the War of 1812. Although many of them went unnoticed, the Civil War's female soldiers were documented in enough newspapers, military records, diaries, and letters—including those written by the women's male comrades—to make it possible for us to examine a few of their extraordinary stories more closely today.

She Went to the Field profiles several substantiated cases of female soldiers during the Civil War, including Sarah Emma Edmonds, aka Private Frank Thompson, Union; Janeta Velazquez, aka Lieutenant Harry T. Buford, Confederate; Sarah Rosetta Wakeman, aka Private Lyons Wakeman, Union; Loreta Jennie Hodgers, aka Private Albert D. J. Cashier, Union; Frances Hook, aka Private Frank Miller, Union; and Frances Clayton, Florena Budwin, Mary Ann Clark, and Mary Pitman. The book also addresses those women who may not have posed as male soldiers but who nonetheless pushed contemporary gender boundaries to act boldly in military capacities as spies, nurses, and vivandières—or "daughters of the regiment"—who bore the flag in battle, rallied troops, and cared for the wounded.

A female soldier enlisted for many of the same reasons that her brother or father might have—"for the sheer adventure and romance of joining the army and seeing places far from home," or to "earn the bounties and pay," as Civil War historian Lauren Cook Burgess notes in her book *An Uncommon Soldier*. In her letters home, Rosetta Wakeman consistently addressed a preoccupation with sending her wages home to pay off family debt. Others joined the ranks out of patriotism, hoping to serve their respective causes: In her 1864 memoirs the Union's Sarah Edmonds stressed her response to the call of duty issued by her adopted country. Loreta Velazquez often wished she were a man so that she

2

could serve the Confederacy and prove her competence as a soldier comparable to her husband. Their personal writings—rare documents of women who fought—also show that Wakeman, Edmonds, and Velazquez all boldly fled from dissatisfying family lives. Each woman's home was restricted to common gender roles, but each woman's flight into the military was precipitated by many of the same reasons that motivated male enlistees.

"How do breeches and coats feel, I wonder," wrote loyal Confederate and Louisiana native Sarah Morgan in a July 1862 journal entry. "I have heard so many girls boast of having worn men's clothes." In profile, women soldiers were young, often poor, and born into farming families—much like the typical male volunteer. Many women on the homefront felt the urge to flee from suffocating situations and daily environments, their existences frequently characterized by discontent, inactivity, and traditional gender constraints. The women mentioned in this book translated those impulses into action.

The stories of Civil War women soldiers are exceptionally difficult to document because of the secrecy they employed to enlist in the war. Many women told no one or only informed a husband or a brother of their plans for fear of losing their reputation or being discharged if discovered. Consequently, the degree to which these stories can be verified varies greatly, and the few available primary sources in letters and memoirs are extremely valuable to a historical discussion of their mobilization for war. Of the sources examined, Rosetta Wakeman's letters are probably the most reliable, because they were written at the time of her military service and without the intent for publication. Sarah Edmonds's memoirs were written in 1864, soon after the end of her military participation. In the initial publication, she does not mention explicitly that her exploits as a nurse and spy took place while she posed as a male soldier in the Second Michigan Volunteers. She wrote as though she worked as a female nurse who only occasionally employed a male disguise for spying missions. Fears about disclosing too much and having rumors taint her reputation kept Edmonds from revealing all her adventures in the war. Not until 1886, when she needed to claim a government pension, did she decide the risk was worth the criticism she might receive. Her memoirs are widely substantiated by her contemporaries and modern-day historians, though recent scholarship by Elizabeth Leonard questions some details of her story.

Loreta Velazquez's memoirs were written eleven years after the end of the war and are perceived to be the most controversial of the three. Historians such as Burgess agree that some incidents in Velazquez's memoirs can be confirmed through other sources but hold the work as a mostly fictionalized account. But other scholars, including DeAnne Blanton, Lauren M. Cook, and Richard Hall, believe that Velazquez's descriptions of her thwarted efforts and defeats tend to, as Hall puts it, "contradict the notion that she was merely trying to tell a good yarn and make herself out to be a heroine for profit." Hall substantiates many of the events in Velazquez's memoirs in his book *Patriots in Disguise*. Edmonds's and Velazquez's are the only published memoirs of women soldiers in army service, and Wakeman's letters are the only known collection of its kind.

Jennie Hodgers was illiterate, but her war and postwar presence as Albert Cashier is extensively documented in military papers, hospital records, and newspaper articles. Surviving primary-source records at the Illinois Veterans Home and word-of-mouth stories kept alive by residents of Saunemin, Illinois, are vital parts of the body of knowledge we have about her today. Projects such as Illinois Alive!, a regional initiative organized by the Alliance Library System, have given the public invaluable access to a digital library of archival resources.

The women who dressed as male soldiers weren't the only ones who left the homefront for the battlefront. Traditional texts may have represented war as a man's fight, says historian Catherine Clinton in a PBS interview for the documentary "The Time of the Lincolns," but besides those women who went as soldiers in disguise, "there were women who served in camps as laundresses. . . [and nurses and cooks] who served in diet kitchens." Prostitution was one reason that female presence in the camps was so controversial—as with many previous wars, Clinton states, "whenever there were large numbers of unattached men, unattached women followed"—but women who headed into the combat zone to work and aid in the resistance helped dispel widespread notions that all females at the front were prostitutes. Kady Brownell followed her husband into the army as a color-bearer for his regiment, rallying troops during battle and administering medical care. Clara Barton collected vast amounts of relief supplies and brought them directly to the wounded soldiers who needed them. Harriet Tubman worked as a scout for Union troops on military expeditions on the South Carolina coast and also joined the ranks as a nurse. In previous war efforts, women primarily prepared food, knitted and sewed clothing and flags, and were permitted to care for soldiers in only a limited medical capacity. But these Civil War women defied convention to lead major organizational and logistical efforts to better sanitary conditions, engage in espionage activities, free slaves, raise morale, and otherwise contribute to the causes they believed in.

Regardless of the details of secret enlistment, the story of the women who fought as soldiers in the American Civil War is a recently rediscovered and valuable ride into history. Examining the Civil War through the lens of these female soldiers offers additional insight on existing historical work. This book is intended as an introduction to the subject, offering brief profiles of a few of these women, as well as sketches of other army women whose actions also demanded a great deal of audacity and nerve. I owe a significant debt to recently expanded scholarship in the field, most importantly to Lauren Cook and Deanne Blanton's exhaustive ten-year documentary work, *They Fought Like Demons: Women Soldiers in the American Civil War.* I hope my own effort will lead readers to find out more. There is much more to know.

Sarah Emma Edmonds

"More than one member of the company can attest . . . Frank's 'manly bearing,' soldierly qualities, kindness, and devotion to the sick deserve to be recognized in a liberal and substantial manner."

—*testimony of Sumner Howard, former member of Second Michigan Regiment, Company F, in a House of Representatives report arguing for Sarah Edmonds's pension on March 22, 1882*

AS A YOUNG GIRL, Sarah Emma Edmonds received a gift: a book championing a heroine named Fanny Campbell who fought on the high seas disguised as a male pirate during the American Revolution. Little did the bearer of the gift know the influence the story would have on Sarah. "I am emancipated!" Sarah thought to herself, her imagination fired by the mere possibility of acting so freely. In her memoirs she would later acknowledge the role Fanny played in liberating her mind from the social constraints of her time: "When I read where 'Fanny' cut off her brown curls and donned the blue jacket and stepped into the freedom and glorious independence of masculinity, I threw up my old straw hat and shouted."

Sarah Emma Edmonds was born in 1841 to a traditional farming

Sarah Emma Edmonds in female attire, and as Franklin Thompson.
CREDIT: STATE ARCHIVES OF MICHIGAN

family in New Brunswick, Canada. For the most part Sarah and her sisters lived the lives of typical nineteenth-century farm girls: They worked outdoors, helped their parents with the planting and harvesting of crops, took care of the horses, milked the cows, chopped wood, and learned to hunt and fish. Though Sarah often fantasized about adventures outside her daily routine, it wasn't until about 1856 that her life took a real detour toward uncharted territory.

Fifteen was a ripe age for marriage—Sarah's own mother had been married at that age. Sarah's flight from her New Brunswick home was precipitated by her father's decision to marry her off to a neighboring farmer much older than herself. "While the preparations were going on for the wedding, one starless night I most unceremoniously left for parts unknown," she later wrote. Sarah made her escape with help from her mother, who understood her feelings against the arrangement. Eventually, Sarah adopted male dress, cut her hair, and took up the name Franklin Thompson in order to facilitate her travels.

As Frank Thompson, Sarah could go to town unchaperoned and stay out as late as she liked. She could eat alone in restaurants—something not taken lightly by women of her time. Farming life had not sated her intellectually, and her thirst for education led her across the border to the northern United States, where she entertained thoughts of entering the field of "foreign missionary." She ended up in New England, working as a successful Bible bookseller and publisher's agent in Hartford, Connecticut. It is unclear whether she posed exclusively as a man during her first five years away from home. What is certain is that her guise gained her meaningful employment at a publishing house, work she could not have secured had she been outfitted in female attire.

Her work for the publisher took Sarah back to Canada and on to Flint, Michigan. One morning in May 1861, as she waited for a train bound for New England, she heard military recruiters calling for enlistees. A voice in the street broke through her reverie and proclaimed, "New York *Herald*—Fall of Fort Sumter—President's Proclamation—Call for seventy-five thousand men!" Images flew up before her eyes of bustling wartime activity—and, of course, the excitement it might bring her. Like her childhood hero Fanny Campbell, Sarah was charged to decide on some kind of action. "The great question to be decided . . . what can I do?" she later wrote. "What part am *I* to act in this great drama?"

As a Canadian, Sarah knew she was not obliged to stay in her adopted country during the American upheaval. But as a deeply religious woman, Sarah thanked God in her memoirs that she was "permitted in this hour of my adopted country's need to express . . . my gratitude which I feel toward the people of the Northern States." Her sense of duty reflected the feelings of many of the men who served as "common soldiers" in the Civil War—though, in the traditional sense, Sarah was far from common.

On May 25, 1861, the beardless young Private Franklin Thompson enlisted with the Flint Union Greys, Company F of the Second Michigan Infantry, a regiment commanded by Colonel Israel B. "Fighting Dick" Richardson. She was twenty years old.

Her real identity as a woman went unsuspected at the time. By all accounts, medical examinations in early-war recruiting processes were notoriously brief and superficial. Though regulations stipulated thorough tests of stripped-down potential recruits—physical investigation of limbs, mental alertness, and eye, ear, and speech capacity—the large influx of soldiers who enlisted prevented much more than a perfunctory look at each one. If their fingers were sufficiently deft in gun handling and their teeth strong enough to tear open what soldiers fondly dubbed a "Minnie ball" cartridge (the minié ball was a relatively new cone-shaped bullet that gave rifles better range and accuracy), most volunteers passed with ease—with plenty of leeway for skillfully masqueraded female combatants such as Sarah Edmonds to sneak through.

By the time she enlisted in the Union army for field nurse duty, Sarah was already well acquainted with her male alter ego in both character and dress. With curly brown hair shorn close to her head, Sarah made a strong-jawed and convincing male soldier, as evidenced in photographs taken at the time. Accustomed to outdoor work, Sarah had more experience than most other women in credibly portraying a man, and her pale complexion had become ruddier with constant exposure to the sun.

A chaotic and emotional scene helped drum up her wartime spirit as she reported to the front lines: the first of the Western troops heading to Washington, D.C., in 1861. Marching bands played with relish their renditions of "The Star-Spangled Banner," while local citizens alternately cheered and wept. In the streets, young soldiers bid their wives and families good-bye. At the start of the Civil War, joining the ranks was a pride-filled occasion. The 1861 volunteer was characteristically confident of a quick resolution to the conflict—in contrast with the reluctant draftees who would come later. The Union soldiers who enlisted alongside Sarah in Michigan, like their counterparts back on the East Coast and across the Confederate lines, were seized by a patriotic fervor and pride in their own ability to obliterate the enemy. In her memoirs Sarah wrote that she was overcome with gratitude that she was free to work for her cause, thus avoiding her feminine obligation "to stay home and weep," in the way that other women in the Union were bound to do.

Soon after Sarah reached the Union capital, she began to tour temporary hospitals set up to accommodate the coming casualties of war. Even then she could see that the U.S. Army's medical department was desperately short-staffed. The United States Sanitary Commission—a volunteer agency to which Sarah would later donate many of the proceeds from her book—was formed in June 1861 to help the government oversee and improve hygienic conditions and medical treatment for its army. But the commission was not yet in full operation to provide sufficient nurses, ambulances, and other crucial hospital supplies. "The troops came pouring in so fast, and the weather being extremely warm, all the general hospitals were soon filled, and it seemed impossible to prepare suitable, or comfortable, accommodations for all who required medical attention," Sarah wrote.

Her observations foreshadowed the difficult and taxing times ahead for army hospital staff. Later in the war, Sarah wrote of her grisly experiences with surgical amputations, often performed by inexperienced crew: "I once saw a young surgeon amputate a limb, and I could think of nothing else than of a Kennebec Yankee whom I once saw carve a Thanksgiving turkey; it was his first attempt . . . and the way in which he disjointed those limbs I shall never forget."

In her efforts to canvas wealthy Georgetown citizens for supplies and food, Sarah was joined by Chaplain and Mrs. B., her "constant companions in hospital labor." Though she never identified them by their full names in her writings, the Chaplain and his wife played a significant role in Sarah's life as a soldier and nurse. Mrs. B., a tall, slender, able-bodied woman with dark hair and blue eyes, was one of the first women to work in the wartime hospitals, particularly on the battlefront. Sarah greatly respected Mrs. B. as her partner in crime at the front lines and would often have reason to admire her friend's fearless actions on the field.

Did Sarah ever think that she, like Mrs. B., could reveal herself as a woman and successfully contribute to the war effort without donning a male soldier's garb? It's important to remember that Mrs. B. was, at the time, a unique exception. Until September 1862's horrific battle of Antietam, which wiped out huge numbers of soldiers, women generally did not work at hospitals but remained at home, sewing flags, uniforms, and even underwear. At Antietam, 5,000 men were killed and more than 26,000 wounded, making it the bloodiest day in American history. It was only after this debacle that women were more actively recruited from their stitching duties to take charge at hospitals as nurses. When she described her feelings in a postwar interview, Sarah's decision to begin her service to the Union in male attire came to a clearer light: "I could better perform the necessary duties for sick and wounded men, and with less embarrassment to them and to myself as a man than as a woman."

Her military contemporaries gave credit to her as Franklin Thompson, who trudged faithfully through the daily muck of camp life. Every dawn witnessed her up at reveille call alongside the men in her regiment. Summer's sweltering heat invited sunstroke and dehydration to the camps, while endless marching outfitted the soldiers in bloodied and blistered feet. June brought typhoid fever, dysentery, diarrhea, and malaria, which Sarah, as a nurse, found harder to fend off than any Confederate battalion. Indeed, many more soldiers died from disease in the Civil War than ever could have been killed by bullets alone; hundreds of thousands more were left crippled in the wake of what has been called the "Third Army."

When the rains came to cool off the sultry Southern summer, Sarah, Mrs. B., and the rest of the hospital staff despaired. Wet ground bred disease, and tents blew down in the high winds, exposing patients to the elements. Sarah watched many of her "noble boys in blue" die in camp before they ever saw a major skirmish.

Despite the obvious obstacles, carrying out her work with determination made Sarah a proud and patriotic missionary and fulfilled her earlier dreams: "I wondered if there ever was a 'Missionary Field' which promised a richer harvest, than the one in which I was already engaged; and oh, how thankful I was that it was my privilege to take some small part in so great a work," she later wrote of those first months of service.

Sarah was initiated into battle at the First Battle of Bull Run (Manassas) on July 21, 1861—the first major military engagement of the war. Her regiment had been situated just outside Washington, D.C., for about a month when General Irvin McDowell ordered three divisions to march south toward the main Confederate army camped in Manassas Junction, Virginia. The evenings before the battle were spent in prayer, which allowed Sarah some measure of peace. "We retired feeling refreshed and encouraged," she wrote.

Spectators present during the early morning of the battle would have seen a vision of quietly marching bodies winding through the verdant hills and valleys of the Virginia countryside, blades glinting. At daybreak the two armies set first sight on each other. As the battle began, Sarah crouched down out of the line of fire with Mrs. B. As the unreal spectacle of war unfolded around her, Sarah fixed her gaze on Mrs. B. for comfort—focusing on her black riding habit, silver-mounted seven-shooter, and water canteen—and tried to prepare mentally for the job at hand. The two women were further armed with flasks of brandy and sacks of provisions, bandages, and adhesive plaster, and would soon need all the supplies they had.

The air was filled that Sunday with the boom of artillery, the "clash of steel" and a "continuous roar of musketry." The tide of battle rolled back and forth over Sarah and Mrs. B., but they darted among fields of "wounded, dead, and dying" and dispensed brandy to the lips of soldiers writhing in agony, limbs askew. Desperate to secure water for the soldiers, the two raced to a spring located a mile from the main battlefront—under a hail of bullets from Confederate sharpshooters intent on making sure their enemies stayed thirsty.

By noon the Confederate troops had retreated to give a fairly confident appearance of a Union victory, though the casualties were dismal. The field seemed to be carpeted with men who waved feebly for aid or lay grimly still. As Sarah tended to them, she had to dodge scattershot that still sprayed in wide arcs through the air.

Two blue-uniformed regiments of fresh troops arrived, and Sarah and her compatriots relaxed, glad to see reinforcements. As the troops came closer, however, they began firing a volley at point-blank range. Assumed to be friendly regiments, the soldiers were actually the Rebel Thirty-third Virginia, outfitted in blue. The confrontation resulted in a widespread panic that sent mobs of Union soldiers fleeing northeast toward the town of Centerville for safety.

In chaos and confusion, which included civilians who had traveled from the capital to watch the battle, Sarah finally made her way back to Centerville and then on to Washington, where the Union forces had retreated. Unable to take along the dead and wounded, the Union army had left them to the advancing enemy. Those who had enough strength made it on their own to one of six woefully ill-prepared hospitals outside the Federal capital, only to face a grim shortage of personnel to care for them.

On her way back to the capital, Sarah encountered wounded and dying soldiers on the road. For as many of the living as she could, she brought water. For the dying, she took their precious letters, lockets, and photos back with her to Washington. Some died in her arms, and she snipped locks of their hair to send back to their families. When she arrived in Washington, she set about the bleak task of writing letters and sending these personal effects home to mothers and wives.

A flood of emotional letters came back in response, many "full of gratitude and kind wishes," as Sarah detailed in her memoirs. "One in particular I cannot read without weeping. It is from Willie's Mother . . . 'Oh, can it be that my Willie will return to me no more? Shall I never see my darling boy again, until I see him clothed in the righteousness of Christ—thank God I shall see him then—I shall see him then.' "

In October 1861 Sarah met Jerome John Robbins at the regimental hospital at Alexandria, Virginia, where she was serving duty and delivering messages to remote hospital branches. She referred to him in her writings as "one of the noble-hearted nurses"; he would soon have a profound effect on her. She noted that she "had the honor of meeting and congratulating him" and "felt that it was a greater honor than to converse with many of our major generals." Jerome, an assistant surgeon and medical steward for the Second Michigan, had been imprisoned by the Rebel army upon his refusal to abandon his patients.

Later freed, he befriended the young Private Thompson. During the long periods in camp, the two soldiers entered into philosophical discussions about human nature, religion, and how life would carry on once the war ended. In an unlikely setting teeming with the messy details of caring for sick and wounded men, Sarah managed to fall in love with Jerome. His perception of Sarah as Frank Thompson was positive in its own right: "How invaluable is the friendship of one true heart," he wrote in his diary.

In November Sarah confessed to Jerome that she was actually a woman, shocking him so much that he wrote a long passage about the experience in his diary, which he promptly sealed. Jerome told Sarah that he already had his own "especial affection" for a girl named Anna in his hometown. Hurt and jealous, Sarah did not succeed in hiding her disappointment. Jerome wrote in his diary that her behavior became "dissagreable [sic]" and she "acts strangely . . . [and] appears very much out of humor." The resulting damage to their relationship was irreparable, though they still remained on friendly terms, at least superficially, for several months.

Apparently Jerome was careful to keep Sarah's secret, not only in person but also in his diary, referring to her as "Frank" or "Thompson" even after he discovered her true identity. Sarah eventually became enamored of Assistant Adjutant General James Reid of the Seventy-ninth New York Infantry, with whom she shared a close relationship. The two did not go unnoticed by Jerome John Robbins, who noted James in his journal as "Frank's particular friend" and Sarah as his "pet." Though they may have been lovers—and testimony from Sarah's contemporaries at the time seems to indicate some evidence of this—

James Reid was married. Sarah Edmonds proved a tough recruit, but apparently she was not completely immune to entanglements with her fellow soldiers.

Despite certain emotional turmoil, Sarah's efforts in the war continued. In her second year of military service, she participated in the largely unsuccessful spring and summer campaign of the Army of the Potomac on the Virginia Peninsula and suffered the Union defeat at Fredericksburg. She "catered for the hospitals," procuring medical supplies and food provisions from nearby Southern plantations—often a dangerous mission, as many Confederate women were understandably hostile to passing Federal troops. One female Rebel Sarah encountered tried to shoot her as she departed her home. In her account of the exchange, Sarah wrote that she shot the woman in the hand in return. According to Sarah, the woman—whom her regiment christened "Nellie"—eventually turned over to the Union cause and became a nurse herself. Tongue-in-cheek, Sarah described Nellie in her memoirs as "the only real lady" she met in the South.

Franklin Thompson's military record also showed letter carrier service from April to July 1862. As a postal carrier Sarah braved long trips on horseback between camps, as well as enemy fire. In December of that year, she served as an orderly to Colonel Orlando Poe, who had replaced "Fighting Dick" Richardson as commander of her regiment. After seeing her in woman's attire at a Second Michigan reunion years later, Colonel Poe wrote that he easily "recall[ed] many things which ought to have betrayed her, except that no one thought of finding a woman in a soldier's dress." Sarah's reliable work apparently spoke volumes without her even saying a word.

Sarah identified strongly with her fellow soldiers, ready at a minute's warning to go into the field of battle and take her stand with the boys. Her brash restlessness for action and desire to put down the enemy showed her strength of character and resolve. As long as she was not discovered, she could continue to be freer than she had ever been alongside her male compatriots.

On the death of Lieutenant James V., a childhood friend from New Brunswick, Sarah described the deep emotional connection she felt with him, resulting from common home and purpose: "There was a strong bond of sympathy existing between us, for we both believed that duty called us there, and were willing to lay down even life itself, if need be, in this glorious cause. Now he was gone, and I was left alone with a deeper sorrow in my heart than I had ever known before." Strikingly, Sarah claimed that her friend never seemed to recognize her while they were together in camp.

Though her military record doesn't indicate spy service, Sarah detailed several such adventures in her memoirs. After tending to an injured Confederate soldier while disguised as an Irish peddler-woman, Sarah's views on the enemy and on her own mortality were altered. "It is strange how sickness and disease disarm our antipathy and remove our prejudices. There lay before me an enemy to the Government for which I was daily and willingly exposing my life . . . [and yet] in his helpless condition, I did not feel the least resentment." The prayers that the enemy soldiers uttered were identical to those of Union soldiers, and Sarah realized that so many of their beliefs and desires were alike. The song "Somebody's Darling" became symbolic of the sense of suffering and loss that Sarah felt as a Union soldier for the other side.

But Sarah did not let the specter of mortality deter her from completing what she envisioned as her duty. Even though she was haunted by visions of Lieutenant James V.'s death, what dominated her mind was the thought of action. Rather than taking care of the sick and wounded as she did at the outset of war, Sarah desired more aggressive duty. Her friend's death spurred her to accept her first spy mission, "with all its fearful responsibilities." Not only did she endure, but she truly enjoyed the adventures—complete with deprivations and hardships—that were connected with her risky spy missions. "Perhaps a spirit of adventure was important," she wrote in her memoirs, "but *patriotism* was the grand secret of my success."

The perils of war, intensified by the pressures of remaining undetected as a female soldier, eventually did get the best of Sarah Emma Edmonds. She deserted in April 1863 after a bout with malaria while her regiment was stationed in Lebanon, Kentucky. The event came as a surprise to her compatriots, who had come to regard young Private Frank Thompson as a "frank and fearless" soldier. Her service record would later indicate that she was a willful and responsible participant in every trial that her regiment faced. Her military colleagues characterized her as a soldier who obeyed "all orders with intelligence and alacrity, his whole aim and desire to render zealous and efficient aid to the Union cause." The reasons for her disappearance are unclear, but Sarah later attributed her departure to illness and to fear of having her true sex disclosed, as she had applied for a leave to seek medical care and been denied. She fled to Washington, D.C., and then headed to Ohio to work as a female hospital nurse—under her own name—with the United States Christian Commission until the end of the war.

Historians such as Elizabeth Leonard have also surmised that Sarah's love for James Reid, who left the army shortly before her desertion, may have also factored in her departure.

From her post as a nurse in Ohio, Sarah returned to Michigan. She refused, however, to resign herself to postwar inactivity. Her memoirs, titled *Unsexed; or, The Female Soldier,* were released in 1864—before the Civil War ended. The following year the book was reissued with a less provocative title, *Nurse and Spy in the Union Army,* and was eventually reprinted again in 1999 as *Memoirs of a Soldier, Nurse, and Spy.* Still relevant 139 years after its first publication in recounting some of the most vicious conflicts of the American Civil War, Sarah Emma Edmonds's memoirs are widely held by historians to tell a substantially true story, cross-referenced with other sources in Sylvia Dannett's detailed biography *She Rode with the Generals.* According to some sources, however, Sarah admitted much later that the memoirs were "not strictly a factual account." Nonetheless, her book eventually sold about 175,000 copies; ever a patriot, she donated its profits (estimated at hundreds and perhaps thousands of dollars) to various soldiers' aid organizations.

In 1867 Sarah married Linus H. Seelye, who also grew up in New Brunswick. The marriage was arguably the closest she would ever come to conventional domestic life. The couple had three children who died early in life, but they later adopted two sons.

Her unusual story revealed to the public, Sarah became a lecturer on her war experiences in 1883. She wrote numerous letters to military personnel and government officials to secure a pension and finance her dream of a soldiers' home. Because her guise was so successful, it was a difficult task to persuade the Veterans and Pension Bureau of the truth. True to her bold nature, she appeared at the 1884 reunion of her former regiment in Flint, Michigan, dressed as a woman. Through House reports and a special act of Congress, Sarah finally gained her pension—the standard $12 a month—and the removal of "deserter" from her military record. She received her back pay and bounty in 1889. The total was $100.

Eventually Sarah and Linus settled in Texas. In 1897 Sarah was mustered in Houston to the George B. McClellan Post of the Grand Army of the Republic (GAR), a Civil War veterans' organization committed to preserving the memory of Union soldier sacrifice—the only woman ever to be thus honored. Sarah Emma Evelyn Edmonds Seelye died September 5, 1898, in La Porte, Texas. In 1901 she was laid to rest again at Houston's Washington Cemetery with full military honors.

Loreta Janeta Velazquez

"Within three days I managed to provide myself with a very complete military outfit; quite sufficient to enable me to commence operations without delay . . . I was exceedingly anxious to carry out a magnificent idea I had in my mind, and to present myself before my husband, under such auspices that he could no longer find an excuse for refusing his consent to my joining the Southern army as a soldier."

—*Loreta Janeta Velazquez, from* The Woman in Battle

ACROSS THE WAR LINES from Sarah Emma Edmonds was Loreta Janeta Velazquez. According to her 1876 memoir, *The Woman in Battle,* she was born in Havana, Cuba, on June 26, 1842, to a Spanish father and a French-American mother and educated by an English governess for much of her early life. Her father's plantation wealth allowed her to travel to New Orleans to complete and perfect her education in English. She lived there with an aunt, who later sent her to a school run by the Sisters of Charity. The dreamy young Loreta spent her allowance on fairy-tale books instead of the usual sweets that most other children preferred.

"I built air-castles without number, and in my daydreams I was fond of imagining myself as the hero of most stupendous adventures," she wrote. "I wished that I could only change places with my brother Josea." The introduction to the volume documents warrior heroines of history whose stories inspired her. One role model, however, was peerless in her eyes. "From my early childhood Joan of Arc was my favorite heroine," she enthused. "Whenever I think of the women who have distinguished themselves in battle, my affections turn to the greatest and noblest of them all, and my imagination fires with a desire to emulate the glorious deeds of Joan of Arc." The praise Loreta lavished upon the Maid of Orlean appropriately matched the passion she felt for war. She described herself in her memoirs as "perfectly wild on the subject of war. I felt that now the great opportunity of my life had arrived." On the basis of historical example, she felt confident in her own ability to contribute to the war effort as well as any man: "When women have rushed to the battlefield they have invariably distinguished themselves."

Like Sarah Edmonds, Loreta Velazquez claimed unhappiness with her early betrothal, to a Spaniard named Raphael. Though she did not initially protest the engagement, the idea of a traditionally arranged "marriage of convenience," as she called it, began to plague her. Threats of being sent to a convent or even back to Cuba notwithstanding, Loreta ultimately eloped with William—a young American army officer—on April 5, 1856, and consequently became estranged from her family. She voiced her frustrations with her parents and their conflict with her own desires when she wrote, "They were mistaken . . . for, like a good many girls, as soon as I was old enough to do much thinking for myself, I had no difficulty in coming to the conclusion that the choice of a husband was something I ought to have a voice in."

A portrait of Loreta Janeta Velazquez.

CREDIT: *THE WOMAN IN BATTLE* (1876)

Loreta's education in New Orleans and her association with American girls factored into the ideological and social separation from her family. America was a "free country," her classmates informed her when they heard of her betrothal, and no girl should have to marry a man without her own consent. The school environment fed a burgeoning rebellion against her old-fashioned Catholic upbringing and against the Spanish tradition of accepting matches made by one's parents.

Like her husband, Loreta joined the Methodist Church and became a Protestant, but she missed her family acutely. As the couple moved from place to place according to William's military appointments, she continued to hope for a reconciliation. Finally, after the birth of her first child, her father consented to a visit. Loreta's mother and brother journeyed to her home in St. Louis, but her father remained cold to Loreta's alliance with an American soldier. According to Loreta, her father had a long history of animosity toward the United States. He had resigned a job with the Spanish government in Cuba to claim a large estate inheritance in Texas, then part of Mexico. When the Mexican-American War began in 1846, the family had been living in San Luis Potosí for only a year. Loreta's father fought as an officer in the Mexican army. Unfortunately for him, the end of the war found the Americans triumphant and his estate decimated. The entire family eventually moved back to Cuba, but he never lost his "bitterness" toward the Americans.

By fall 1860 Loreta wrote in her memoir that her three children had died, either of fever or shortly after childbirth, and she distracted herself with the coming military conflict between the North and South. The talk of war stirred up her childhood impulse to dress as a man and participate in her own glorious hero fantasies by joining her husband in combat. Having been a loyal United States military man for so long, her husband William had his doubts about the wisdom of secession. But with her own desire for adventure coupled with a Confederate fervor, Loreta added to the familial pressure already put upon William to depart for Richmond and join the Southern troops.

According to Loreta, her first foray into male guise—complete with false mustache, wig, and one of William's suits—was accomplished in the company of her husband in Memphis, Tennessee, shortly before his departure to the Confederate capital for service. To prove to his wife the coarseness and generally "demoralizing" environment of men in camp, and to dissuade her from following him to the battlefield, William agreed to a nighttime excursion to the bars, saloons, and gambling venues of the city. Without the moderating influence of "decent women," William informed her, men were nothing short of rude and intolerable. Instead of dissuading Loreta, however, the experience showed her how possible it was to masquerade successfully as a male. The "loud-talking, hard-drinking, and blaspheming" souls she witnessed only strengthened her resolve to be a good soldier and put them to shame. Tellingly, she longed to be an "actor" in the war, which she initially saw as a "sublime, living drama."

Loreta viewed the conflict between the North and South as her own glorious opportunity to accomplish something great, and she focused on the possibilities of independence that came along with playing a male role. Not viewing her masquerade as a deception, she expected William to welcome her upon their next encounter. "I waited impatiently for him to leave," wrote Loreta of her husband, contriving to "give him a genuine surprise when next we met, and to show him that his wife was as good a soldier as he, and was bent upon doing as much or more for the cause which both had at heart."

Loreta described the use of wire contraptions custom-made by a tailor to flatten and thicken her feminine figure and how she cleverly avoided having her face shaved by the barber when getting her hair cut in the masculine fashion of the day. At enlistment, many men were young and unbearded. The median age of Civil War soldiers was just under twenty-six, with many boys in their teens upon recruitment, so it was not unusual to have smooth-faced youngsters in the ranks. "So many men have weak and feminine voices," noted Loreta, "that provided the clothing is properly constructed and put on right . . . a woman with even a very high-pitched voice need have very little to fear on that score." Her getup was apparently so convincing that later on in her military career, she claimed to become the object of many women's affections when she went out in society; chapters with such subtitles as "A Lesson in Courtship," "A Bit of Flirtation with a Columbia Belle," and "Another Lady in Love with Me" showed up in her book, and not without controversy. In 1878 Confederate general Jubal Early, outraged at the depiction of Loreta's immoral behavior in *The Woman in Battle*, wrote an angry diatribe to Congressman W. F. Slemons of Arkansas, stating that she was "no type of Southern woman."

It was after she got herself outfitted with a trunk of clothing that Loreta adopted the identity of Lieutenant Harry T. Buford. She planned to raise and equip her own battalion and meet her husband on the field. She detailed the improbable story of successfully raising 236 men in four days for what she fondly called her troop of "Arkansas Grays." But soon after she reached William in Pensacola, she wrote, he was killed in an accident while demonstrating how to use a carbine. After his death, she gave up her battalion to seek work as an independent soldier, claiming to have met with Brigadier General Bonham before the First Battle of Bull Run to obtain an assignment.

In *The Woman in Battle*, Loreta described waking up at dawn on the morning of Bull Run. The heat of the morning built up in a

An illustration of Loreta Velazquez in uniform as Lieutenant Harry T. Buford.
CREDIT: *THE WOMAN IN BATTLE* (1876)

cloudless blue sky, and her eagerness to fight rose with the sun. Though she "labored under some disadvantages in not having a regular commission, and not being attached to a regular command," she believed that she then had a better opportunity to choose a position in battle and "distinguish" herself as a hero. She was intent on showing her fellow soldiers that she was "as good a man as any one of them." Despite her "petite" figure, she was more than convinced of her ability to put up good fight for the Confederacy.

If her story is true, then Loreta Velazquez's battlefield rite of passage came on the same day as that of Sarah Emma Edmonds, at the First Battle of Bull Run. Loreta described the approach of the Yankee troops as one that "could be distinctly traced by the clouds of dust raised by the tramping of thousands of feet, and, once in a great while, the gleam of the bayonets was discerned." The "incessant tumult," the haze of dust and smoke, the deafening sounds of artillery fire—to Loreta all were earmarks of that day, and the details she provided were similar to Sarah Edmonds's account of the battle. But, unlike Sarah's memoir, Loreta's book painted a particularly dashing portrait of herself in the hero's role, having taken over the lead of a company whose commander had just been lost: "The desire to avenge my slaughtered comrades, the salvation of the cause which I had espoused, all inspired me to do my utmost; and no man on the field that day fought with more energy or determination than the woman who figured as Lieutenant Harry T. Buford," she wrote of that first combat experience.

When it comes to her specific exploits and actual participation in battle, many Civil War scholars believe that Loreta Janeta Velazquez's story was significantly exaggerated for her audience's reading pleasure. In her memoir she details a series of adventures and involvements in specific battles, including Ball's Bluff, the attack at Fort Donelson, and the bloody encounter at Shiloh, where close to 24,000 soldiers were killed, wounded, or missing. She claimed that after having her gender discovered twice, she persistently reenlisted and eventually became a spy under the name of "Mrs. Williams," and she mentioned involvement in an astounding variety of scouting and detective activities while working as a double agent for the Confederate Secret Service.

Throwing more than a shadow of doubt on the entire account is the fact that the name Lieutenant Harry T. Buford never appeared in official military records from the war—a fact Loreta accounted for by her "independent" status as a lieutenant who raised her own forces. Historian Elizabeth Leonard, in her pivotal work *All the Daring of the Soldier*, characterizes *The Woman in Battle* as a kind of fictionalized memoir on which editor and publisher C. J. Worthington worked substantially, "refining Velazquez's prose for a popular audience and having corrected certain errors of detail. Both Velazquez and Worthington, therefore, confessed up front that *The Woman in Battle* was not a pure memoir per se . . . but rather a product of their combined efforts." As Leonard sees it, the apocryphal nature of the work is due in large part to this collaboration.

Despite the inconsistencies of *The Woman in Battle*, most historians concede some basis of truth for the account and for the existence of Loreta Janeta Velazquez. In her essay on Velazquez for *American National Biography*, Lyde Cullen Sizer states that though Loreta's "more fantastic experiences cannot be corroborated, her narrative is remarkably accurate in recording fairly minute details about weather, commanding officers, and the course of battles." In his book *Patriots in Disguise*, Richard Hall cites Richmond newspaper articles that seem to coincide with particular events in Velazquez's book. The July 4, 1863, issue of the Lynchburg *Daily Virginian*, for example, picked up a report in the Richmond *Enquirer* on the arrest of a woman in Confederate soldier's uniform using the name "Lieutenant Bensford." Furthermore, the woman told police that her name was "Mrs. Alice Williams," a pseudonym that Velazquez supposedly used to spy for the

Confederacy. Even Leonard offers some substantiation that *The Woman in Battle* may have been "rooted in real experience." In *All the Daring of the Soldier,* Leonard states that a request for an officer's commission on July 27, 1863, from a soldier named "H. T. Buford"—Velazquez's pseudonym—was found referenced in the Records of the Confederate Secretary of War. Leonard also notes that evidence in the *Official Records of the Union and Confederate Armies* lends "credence to at least the basic outlines of author Velazquez's claims in *The Woman in Battle.*" Various letters and memos show the employment of an Alice Williams as some kind of "special agent" and that she "received a commission in the Confederate Army as Lieutenant Buford." After the war, in 1867, the New Orleans *Picayune* reports on a Mrs. Mary DeCaulp—though her memoir refers to the existence of several husbands, the only one Loreta names in full is Thomas DeCaulp—who was then an agent for a Venezuelan emigration company and purportedly fought in the war as "Lieutenant Bufort."

Though the veracity of Loreta Janeta Velazquez's chronicled adventures may be in question, the very writing of her memoirs is a daring exploit and extraordinarily revealing of contemporary attitudes and thoughts on the conflict between the North and South. Because of her hopes that war would free her from the confines of traditional womanly duties, Loreta was often entertained by the romantic notion of battle as a "pleasant holiday excursion," rather than the serious and bloody business it was. Not unlike her male comrades in arms, she was glad of any excuse to get away from a dismal home life and thought that fighting the Yankees would be "good fun." Her account is authentic in that she, too, suffered from the illusions of grandeur and overconfidence that ultimately proved fatal to the Southern cause once daydreams of battle became reality.

Many women were genuinely unhappy with the gender constraints that kept them from taking more direct action in the war effort. "It was a feverish desire to be in motion, to be doing something, to have occupation for mind and body" that spurred Loreta to undertake the missions she did. Like the male soldiers who fought at her side, she had invested her "heart and soul" and some of the best years of her life. In a slaveholding society, in a time when America was far from allowing equal freedoms for the country's women, female soldiers seized the opportunity war gave them to taste independence. "For all of its horrors, war has historically offered human beings an opportunity to transcend the limitations of ordinary life," stated the introduction to "Women and War," a 2002 photography exhibit at the Radcliffe Institute's Schlesinger Library, Harvard University. "As men are drawn to such opportunities, so are women."

The additional danger of being caught added to Loreta Velazquez's cooling enthusiasm for the war. Her fantasy of becoming a second Joan of Arc proved to be a girlish fancy. Like those of many of her fellow soldiers, Loreta's views on the battle between North and South became increasingly fatalistic. Her book professed to recognize the mistakes that soldiers—including herself—had made in underestimating the magnitude of war and the real mission they had before them. Although the will to fight was strong on both sides at the outset of war, morale waned as the conflict dragged on. The South in particular was challenged in its dedication to the fight. Historian Reid Mitchell notes that one in four white men of military age died in the South compared with the North's figure of one in ten. Total Union deaths are estimated at about 364,400, including those suffered in combat, disease, and prison, with 277,400 wounded. The Confederate death toll rang in at about 234,000, with approximately 195,000 wounded. The magnitude of the loss dealt a serious blow to the less-populous Southern home front.

After her military adventures ended, Loreta Velazquez traveled with her brother to Europe and made subsequent trips to South America and the western United States. Published in 1876, *The Woman in Battle* immediately became a sensation, but not always a positive one. Loreta was criticized for intentionally trying to make a profit from the war, and Leonard notes that the book was quickly "met with serious challenge," specifically with regard to its authenticity.

The memoirs of Sarah Edmonds and Loreta Velazquez were both written for an audience, with publisher's and editor's prefaces that ask readers to excuse many of the authors' actions. This functions as yet another indication of the atmosphere that surrounded these female soldiers. The author's preface to *The Woman in Battle,* for instance, indicated that Loreta Velazquez was well aware of how her book might be received: "I do not know what the good people who will read this book will think of me. My career has differed materially from that of most women; and some things that I have done have shocked persons for whom I have every respect, however much my ideas of propriety may differ from theirs . . . in my opinion there was nothing essentially improper in my putting on the uniform of a Confederate officer for the purpose of taking an active part in the war." Furthermore, she asserted that "I feel that I have nothing to be ashamed of." For female soldiers like Sarah Edmonds and Loreta Velazquez, the fear of being returned to a passive female existence showed itself to be the most powerful motivator. As illustrated in their personal writings, their chief preoccupations while participating in the war concerned not death but discovery and the prospect of being returned home. Once out of the military ranks that had blurred distinctions for them as women, these former soldiers were once again required by society to be reinserted to their "proper" positions.

By exploring these women's motivations for enlisting—what they thought they could achieve, their changing attitudes toward war, and their positions in the social world—one can acquire a new perspective on the revolutions that were still to come. Seen in context with their fellow, male combatants and home-front women, female soldiers shed a different light on the mindset of women during the Civil War era.

Sarah Rosetta Wakeman

"I feel perfectly happy. If I go into a battle I shall be alright. It is what I have wish[ed] for a good while. . . . If it is God['s] will for me to be killed here, it is my will to die."

—*letter from Rosetta Wakeman to her family, dated April 13, 1863*

THE MAJORITY OF FEMALE—as well as male—Civil War soldiers came from a rural, agrarian background. Many were poor and looking for a better life (high-society girls would have had better prospects and education, thus the soldiering life would not have held much allure for them). Sarah Rosetta Wakeman certainly was representative of these quintessentially poor and less educated soldiers. Born January 16, 1843, she was the eldest of nine children—seven girls and two boys—to Harvey Anable and Emily Hale Wakeman. The family lived in Bainbridge in upstate New York's Chenango County. In 1857 the half of the town in which they resided became the town of Afton. A farming community on the Susquehanna River not far from Binghamton, Afton was primarily a cow town where most farmers relied on dairy production for their livelihood.

The conditions in which she grew up contributed to Rosetta's decision to enlist. A devoted and loving daughter, Rosetta—in her female life, she went by her middle name—did attend some school through her childhood, but for the most part she worked with her family on their farm. Historian Lauren Cook Burgess, in her introduction to *An Uncommon Soldier: The Civil War Letters of Sarah Rosetta Wakeman, alias Pvt. Lyons Wakeman, 153rd Regiment, New York State Volunteers, 1862–1864*, speculates that Rosetta, "being the eldest in a family whose first male child was elementary school age," was the primary helper to her father in his business and might have even become "accustomed to wearing male clothes working on the farm." When Rosetta was seventeen, the 1860 census listed her occupation as a "domestic." Rosetta was concerned with her family's debt, and her job probably did not add significantly to their total income.

Two years later, as Burgess describes in *An Uncommon Soldier*, Rosetta didn't seem to have any prospective suitors for marriage, "which would have relieved the family of her care" and the financial pressures of supporting her. It is probable that she felt the weight of her own burden—the letters she later wrote to her parents were candid about the influence of money on her motivation to leave home. She described her desire to help provide for her family as the most pressing on her mind. Her instructions for using her paychecks were clear and practical, but her tone was wistful: "All the money i send you i want you should spend it for the family in clothing or something to wear. . . . If i ever return i shall have money enough for my self and to divide with you."

In late summer 1862, nineteen-year-old Rosetta left home to begin her life as a "man." At first she went to work briefly in the town of Binghamton before finding employment as a coal handler on a barge

Photo of Sarah Rosetta Wakeman in Union soldier's uniform as Private Lyons Wakeman. CREDIT: THE MINERVA CENTER, INC., FROM *AN UNCOMMON SOLDIER*

that traveled the Chenango Canal. The immediate circumstances of her departure remain unclear, although her letters indicate a possible family feud; her written words provide evidence of estrangement and strained relations with her family. She consistently asked for forgiveness for the "old affray." The question of her status in the family is complicated by ambiguous passages, such as in this December 23, 1862, letter: "I want you should forgive me of everything that I ever done, and I will forgive you all the same." Rosetta's earnest efforts to repair relations from afar continued throughout her two years in the army.

By the end of her first trip as a boatman, she'd met recruiters for the 153rd New York State Volunteers. Instead of continuing on from Canajoharie, a town in Montgomery County, Rosetta decided to enlist as a private with Company H of the 153rd on August 30, 1862, in Fonda, New York—as twenty-one-year-old Lyons Wakeman. "When I got there i saw some soldiers," she wrote to her family in her first letter home. "They wanted I should enlist and so i did. I got 100 and 52$ in money." Certainly a major factor in Rosetta's decision to enlist, the $152 bounty would have been more than a year's income, says Burgess. Even in the guise of a man and receiving payment for work appropriate to her new station in life, Rosetta would have struggled to make that level of salary in any other occupation. In this, she was not unlike male soldiers; the reward of enlistment bounties and payment was one of their primary motivations as well. Bound to the army for three years or for the duration of the war, she and the other enlistees stayed in Montgomery County while recruiters continued to fill out the regiment.

In October the 153rd was finally mustered into service. The troops left for Washington, D.C., on October 18 to perform provost marshal and guard duty at the nation's capital. At a mere 5 feet tall, blue-eyed Lyons Wakeman had fair skin and brown hair and cut a diminutive figure in uniform. But Rosetta was accustomed to physical labor, and her inexperience with military life probably proved less a hindrance than she might have anticipated. Many young men who enlisted in the Civil

War had never held a gun before, and some of their volunteer officers were almost equally as inexperienced. Though the troops did drill in preparation for combat—several hours every day—and marched intensively when they had to engage the enemy, army life for the most part was not strenuous by any means. Much of each day was spent fighting off a deadly threat of a different sort: boredom. According to *The Civil War Society's Encyclopedia of the Civil War*, the "tedium of camp life led the men to find recreational outlets. . . when not drilling or standing guard, the troops read, wrote letters to their loved ones, and played any game they could devise, including baseball, cards, boxing matches, and cockfights." The less-than-rigorous routine made it easier for women soldiers to complete a successful masquerade in camp.

In Alexandria, Virginia, across the Potomac River from Washington, Rosetta and her regiment lived in tents and, like typical soldiers, washed in rivers and attended to other personal matters in the outdoors. In *All the Daring of the Soldier*, Elizabeth Leonard explains that the structure of "camp life, although intimate in some ways," gave women some leeway to deal with personal matters. "Civil War soldiers lived and slept in close proximity to one another, but they rarely changed their clothes . . . [and] passed the bulk of their time, day and night, out of doors, where they also attended to their bodily needs." In her first experience in camp, Rosetta thrived on the physical challenge. "The weather is cold and the ground is froze hard, but I sleep as warm in the tents as I would in a good bed," wrote Rosetta in the winter of 1862–63. The soldiers laid wooden boards down on the ground as a makeshift floor, upon which they often ate with the tin dishes and utensils parceled out to each by the U.S. government. Despite it all,

Rosetta was happy: "I like to be a soldier very well."

Camp life could be more treacherous than battle itself. Only a few months into her term of enlistment, Rosetta wrote home about an epidemic of measles that had felled about thirty in her regiment. Though the troops were vaccinated in December 1862 for smallpox, Rosetta was diagnosed with "Rubeola," or measles, the following month. Burgess notes that Rosetta may have acquired a "mild case of smallpox due to the crude vaccination practices of the day." Leonard points out that Rosetta was lucky to have escaped having her sex discovered during her illness, an oversight that can probably be attributed to the mild strain from which she seemed to have suffered. During the course of the war, disease killed twice the number of white soldiers who died in combat. According to eminent Civil War historian Drew Gilpin Faust, the numbers can be explained by the sheer size of armies and their camps; coming from rural backgrounds, most soldiers "had little exposure to pathogens." The amassing of so many people together in the army camps, she says, "created breeding grounds for disease." Some men also enjoyed the pleasures of visiting prostitutes, who followed troop movements by the thousands; these encounters led to frequent outbreaks of venereal disease.

As the war progressed, Rosetta's experiences made her bolder and more independent in character, and the tone of her letters reflected that shift. "I can tell you what made me leave home. It was because I had got tired of stay[ing] in that neighborhood. I knew that I Could help you more to leave home than to stay there with you," she wrote to her parents. "I am not sorry that I left you. I believe that it will be all for the best yet . . . . When I get out of this war I will come home and see you but I Shall not stay long before I shall be off to take care of my Self." She regularly mentioned that she was "contented" and begged her father not to worry about her. She even described herself as having grown "fat as a hog" and told him earnestly that being a soldier agreed with her "first rate." Certainly she continued to express concern over her family's debt, but while her decision to leave home was influenced by money, there was also a growing sense of her desire to *continue* to stay away—the camp and battlefield were places where she felt strong and significant and where she could perform meaningful duty.

For Rosetta the war was a valuable way to be on her own and to make herself useful. "I [am] enjoying my Self better this summer than I ever did before in this world," she wrote from Alexandria on June 5, 1863. "I don't want you to mourn about me for I can take care of my Self and I know my business as well as other folks know them for me." Stubborn and strong willed, Rosetta experienced a thrill with the freedom that the soldiering life gave her and celebrated the fact that she could act as she liked without regard for anyone else (like any other good soldier, she used a lot of tobacco, believing it would help ward off illness). She made it clear that she alone would make the decisions about her lifestyle, as untraditional as it might have been: "I will Dress as I am a mind to for all anyone else [cares], and if they don't let me Alone they will be sorry for it." For Civil War–era women, public work or service was usually limited to hospital, church, and charity efforts. Refusing to participate in mundane homefront activities that more often than not involved relief-effort sewing circles, Rosetta made a conscious decision to strike out on her own and, in the process, left her family behind.

Rosetta's regular letters home provide a record of her two years' military service for the Union. It's true that her original letters were lacking in punctuation (Burgess performed a valuable historical service by editing, clarifying, and footnoting Rosetta's correspondence in *An Uncommon Soldier*), but despite her limited education, Rosetta was able to communicate legibly. The notes—some of them briefly and casually documenting her daily life, others awkwardly showing a yearning to acknowledge the meaning behind the war's events and her troubled relationship with her family—depict an uncertainty with her changing role. She often wrote to her father inquiring about the farm and the family's welfare, and she often struggled in her conversational efforts: "What do you think of this war? I think I shall have to stay my three years in the army. I can't think of any thing more to Write." She signed her letters "Rosetta" until December 1863, when she began using the pseudonym "Edwin R."; in one letter, dated March 8, 1864, she even scratched over "Rosetta" with "Edwin"—a revealing statement about the continuing conflict she felt about her identity.

For their part of the exchange, her family sent letters, enclosing extra postage stamps (it was sometimes difficult for Rosetta to acquire stamps in camp, as many things cost "double what it is worth") and such comforts as knit gloves, mittens, yarn, and needles. To break up a monotonous camp diet, Rosetta requested apples and bottles of cider, as well as dried beef. Because Rosetta's regiment tended to stay in one place for several months—they camped at Alexandria, Virginia, and Washington, D.C.'s, Capitol Hill before marching on to Louisiana—and because she was religious about sending them her forwarding address, she seemed to receive her family's letters with regularity.

Photography, though around for just over twenty years at the time of the Civil War, also became involved in the correspondence. The Library of Congress estimates that in the years 1860 to 1865, Civil War photographers took about one million photographs. Most of those pictures were taken by Northern photographers; the South lacked the resources to document the conflict in such breadth. While away from home, Rosetta had her "likeness" taken several times—it cost only about 50 cents, as Rosetta wrote to her sister, Celestia, in an April 30, 1863, letter that included one of her photos—and sent home to her family. In an undated letter she inquired about her family's opinion of her appearance: "How do you like the looks of my likeness? Do you think I look better than I did when I was to home?" In asking, she evidently hoped for some kind of approval. The surviving photo of Rosetta Wakeman is a daguerrotype depicting her in Union soldier attire, armed and standing at attention. *Carte de visite* (or "visiting card") photographs eventually became popular among soldiers and the most popular technique of Civil War photography. They were small photographic portraits printed on paper and used as social calling cards, which relatives or friends could exchange during visits or through the mail.

Recruiting became much more difficult as the years passed and volunteer enthusiasm dried up. The Union passed its First Conscription Act in March 1863. In July 1863 the New York City draft riots took place in protest. From her post in Alexandria, Rosetta wrote to her father: "What do you think about that draft in [New] york State? Do you think that you will be drafted or not? I would like to know in you [sic] next letter . . . . If you are drafted I want you to come into my regiment and my Co. if you Can." Patriotically, she added that she hoped the governor would put down the riots and continue the draft of desperately needed soldiers. At the end of July, the 153rd Regiment was transferred to Washington, D.C., to defend against similar riots that were expected there.

In Washington, Rosetta and her company resided in two-story military barracks—sleeping and eating quarters that were a marked improvement over their previous post in Alexandria. The troops were stationed on Capitol Hill, and Rosetta was awed by the grandeur of the Capitol: "We are Right in sight of the united states Capitol. It is one hundred feet high. . . . This building is made all of marble stones. I have been inside of it. I have been in the Congress hall. This is a pretty place you better believe."

At this point Rosetta and her regiment still had not seen battle, and her bravado showed it. "I don't know how long before i shall have to go into the field of battle. For my part i don't care. I don't feel afraid to go. I don't believe there are any Rebel's bullet made for me yet." She continued to revel in her autonomy, and she was buoyed by pride at being a part of the Union army. In the same letter she boasted, "I am as independent as a hog on ice."

In a remarkable turn of events, Rosetta began standing guard at Washington's Carroll Prison, which included three women among its inmates. "One of them," she wrote to her family during her tenure as a guard, "was a Major in the union army and she went into battle with her men." The unidentified woman, Rosetta added, led her troops on horseback "when the Rebel bullets was acoming like a hail storm . . . Now She is in Prison for not doing accordingly to the regulation of

46

war." Rosetta also wrote about two Confederate female spies, who, according to Burgess in her analysis of prisoner records at Carroll Prison, were probably the notorious Belle Boyd (who spied for Major General Stonewall Jackson; see "Spies" chapter) and her prison roommate, Ida P. (who was charged with being a mail carrier for the Confederacy). Rosetta's tone in describing the women was somewhat admiring; although she mentioned that they were caught for being Rebel spies, she also wrote that they were "Smart looking women and [have] good education." That other female contemporaries had the same idea as hers—to work in the guise of a man for a patriotic and military cause—must have been of some comfort or interest to Rosetta. The irony could not have been lost on her: She, a female major masquerading as a male soldier, stood guard over a female major arrested for attempting the same feat.

In Georgetown on October 13, 1863, Rosetta visited friends in the 109th New York State Volunteers—friends she knew from her prior life at home. According to Burgess in *An Uncommon Soldier*, Private Perry Albert Wilder was Rosetta's second cousin, while Sergeant William Henry Austin was a friend about whom she often inquired in her letters home. The meeting with Perry and Henry, as Rosetta referred to them, indicated that the Wakemans didn't keep their eldest daughter's masquerade a secret from neighbors in their community. Rosetta's letter also hinted at this: "They knew me just as Soon as they see me." Burgess speculates that "Rosetta probably visited her friends from home while attired in uniform. Thus Austin and Wilder were two more people added to a widening circle of family and friends who knew that she was serving in the army under an assumed male identity." Her cousin Frank Roberts was a soldier in the Sixty-fourth New York State Volunteers. In addition to corresponding with Rosetta during the course of the war, he wrote letters to the Wakemans referring to Rosetta as "Edwin."

A soldier's life had its moments of despair, and Rosetta felt the strain toward the close of the war. Like other soldiers in combat, she suffered from failing morale as the conflict wore on. In an October 31, 1863, letter addressed to her mother and father, she stated morosely, "It is but one Chance to ten that I ever Shall meet you again in this world." In his analysis of the quintessential Billy Yank and Johnny Reb, historian Bell Irvin Wiley wrote that the initial "flood tide of enthusiasm was destined to be short-lived . . . the spirit of the fighting forces drooped markedly after a few months of conflict and thereafter rose and fell periodically until the end of the war." As the winter of 1863–64 approached, morale was at a low point in the cycle due to setbacks at Chickamauga and the raw tenacity of the Confederate troops.

Yet despite the fatalism that she exhibited alongside her fellow soldiers, Rosetta showed blithe acceptance of the wartime perils that came with her enlistment in the Union army. She trusted her faith to keep her safe. "Wakeman's letters indicate that her religious faith proved a significant source of comfort to her as she contemplated the dangers that her otherwise enjoyable job entailed," writes Leonard in *All the Daring of the Soldier.* Rosetta found escape from the stagnation at home in her soldier's uniform, and her increasing self-satisfaction became more evident as her term of service progressed. She expressed that "for my part I don't Care how long [the war] does last." Her success with the soldier's life showed that she was more than capable of supporting herself. Rosetta wished to tackle postwar adventures in the Western frontier and thought about new careers: "If I ever own a farm It will be in Wisconsin. On the Prairie." Leonard speculates that the spotted calf Rosetta asked her family to take care of in her absence was an animal "which she perhaps intended to be the centerpiece of a farm of her own after the war."

It was February 1864 before Rosetta would see any real battle with her regiment. The 153rd New York State Volunteers left Washington, D.C., on the evening of February 18, marching to Alexandria and then boarding a steamship down the Mississippi River to New Orleans. They joined the First Brigade, First Division, Nineteenth Army Corps, led by Major General Nathaniel P. Banks. Over the next several weeks, the regiment marched northwest to take part in the Red River Campaign in support of the Nineteenth Army Corps. On April 9, 1864, Rosetta Wakeman withstood the four-hour onslaught of Confederate artillery and infantry fire and fought successfully on the front lines with her unit at Pleasant Hill, Louisiana. She lay on the battlefield that night waiting for safety. On April 14, 1864, Rosetta wrote her final letter home. "There was three wounded in my Co. and one killed . . . I feel thankful to God that he spared my life and I pray to him that he will lead me safe through the field of battle and that I may return safe home."

A short time later, Rosetta Wakeman succumbed to illness, which accounted for the majority of soldiers' deaths in the Civil War. She died of chronic diarrhea on June 19, 1864, one of 160 enlistees killed by disease in the 153rd New York Infantry Regiment. How she escaped detection as a woman during her stay at Marine U.S.A.

General Hospital is unclear, but none of her paperwork indicated that she was discovered to be other than a man. Her army discharge certified her death and proclaimed her as having "served HONESTLY and FAITHFULLY with his Company in the field . . ." She was buried as Lyons Wakeman with full military honors in Chalmette National Cemetery in New Orleans.

For the most part, Rosetta Wakeman greatly enjoyed the freedom and the sense of independence that came of her participation as a soldier. Though she never stopped reassuring her family that she cared very much for them, her letters seemed to illustrate an increasing rejection of the behavior formerly expected of her as a woman. According to Burgess, Rosetta's family referred to her as a "brother" after the war to avoid a "long and difficult explanation." The 1865 New York State Census in Chenango County reported twenty-one-year-old Lyons Wakeman among the casualties of war.

Sarah Rosetta Wakeman left behind a firsthand record, a collection of letters written to her family that is all the more valuable to historians because it was created without intent for public consumption. Brought to the outside world more than a century later, the letters had been "preserved in an attic . . . by family members who considered her somewhat of a black sheep and her adventures in male attire a bit strange," says Burgess. The original letters, along with a photograph of her in the army and a ring, remain in the care of family descendants.

Jennie Hodgers

AKA PRIVATE ALBERT D. J. CASHIER, UNION

"During the war Cashier's comrades noted that the handsome young 'Irishman' was rather inclined to be offish, but overlooked the soldier's exclusiveness in their admiration for 'his' military bearing and reckless daring. Often, it is related, Cashier was selected by Capt. Bush for foraging and skirmishing. Owing to the soldier's rigorous health and apparent abandon Cashier was always among those chosen when dependable men were absolutely necessary."

—from an undated newspaper article, Illinois Veterans Home

EVEN DURING THEIR OWN TIME, female soldiers in the Civil War were no secret. The stories of several women combatants were revealed in newspaper accounts and obituaries, though often without much factual detail. Fantastic true-to-life tales continued to emerge in the postwar decades: In 1911 sixty-seven-year-old Civil War veteran Albert D. J. Cashier was revealed as a woman—Jennie Hodgers—when "he" underwent medical examination for a broken leg. After living for a half century as a man, the Irish immigrant was eventually admitted to the Illinois Soldiers' and Sailors' Home in Quincy. A 1914 article in the Quincy *Whig* documents a reporter's visit with Jennie Hodgers at the home, shortly before her move to the state mental hospital: "The little woman does not know that the story of her secret has now been chronicled in every newspaper over the country and is still of the belief that Colonel Anderson and one or two attachés of the hospital, together with ex-Senator [Ira] Lish, are the only ones who know that she is a womn [sic] . . . Colonel Anderson referred to Cashier in her presence as the smallest soldier that served in the Civil war. The reference seemed to please her . . ."

A petite girl of slight build, Jennie Hodgers was born in Clogher Head, Ireland, on December 25, circa 1843. Before the Civil War began, she lived and worked in Illinois for several years under the identity of Albert Cashier. In July 1862 President Abraham Lincoln called for an additional 300,000 troops, and Jennie was one of the volunteers who joined the war effort. In the conflict's second year, it became increasingly apparent that more men were needed and that the battle between North and South would last longer than anyone had previously thought. In the Belvidere recruiting office of Boone County, Illinois, a farming area straddling the Kishwaukee River, Private First Class Cashier enlisted for a three-year term on August 6, 1862—proudly becoming an official member of the Ninety-fifth Illinois Infantry Volunteers, Company G. The regiment would go on to become one of the hardest-fighting units in the war, suffering some of the greatest casualties and logging about 9,000 miles during its term.

Elizabeth Leonard suggests that Jennie may have first worn boy's clothing as a child while helping her father tend sheep in Ireland. After her arrival in the United States (probably as a teenage stowaway), she continued living in the dress and identity of a boy so that she could

A photograph of Irish-born Jennie Hodgers as Private Albert D. J. Cashier.
CREDIT: ILLINOIS STATE HISTORICAL LIBRARY

get work in a shoe factory. Like many other young recruits in the ranks, Jennie was illiterate, but, even without the ability to read or write, she enlisted—using an "X" as her mark on all authorized documents that demanded her signature—and kept updated on the war through word of mouth. Her company descriptive book listed her as a nineteen-year-old farmer from New York City, 5 feet 3 inches tall, with auburn hair, blue eyes, and a fair complexion. A tintype photograph of Jennie Hodgers as Albert Cashier can be viewed at the Gilder Lehrman Collection at New York's Pierpoint Morgan Library. The black-and-white portrait was taken of Jennie and a bearded fellow soldier during the war. The exact date of the portrait is unknown, but it appears to have been shot in a photographer's studio with a blanket and backdrop. Jennie looks every bit the part of the male soldier, with short, flyaway hair and a firm set of mouth and jaw—though small, she is a convincing and solid figure in uniform. It is not at all apparent from the image that she is a woman. Her clear, light eyes look unwaveringly at the camera, and her body leans slightly toward her companion in the frame, perhaps indicating a close friendship. Both soldiers are somber faced, seated with legs crossed and hands folded. Introduced in the early 1850s, the tintype was one popular kind of photograph technique used to document the Civil War, mostly because the photographs it made were fairly inexpensive, produced on a thin tin plate, and could be sent to family through the postal service. The process made one-of-a-kind reverse (or mirror) images of the subject. Like many other tintypes from the time, this one was set in a framed leather-bound case lined with crimson velvet and covered in glass. The protective leather case, with hook closures, has textured ornate designs cut into it.

After enlistment, Jennie Hodgers mustered into service and trained with her regiment for two months at Camp Fuller in Rockford, Illinois, before departing for Jackson, Tennessee, to serve under Major General Ulysses S. Grant's command in the Central Mississippi campaign. At a time in the war when few battles were being won by the

Union, General Grant began a run of victories in the West that ultimately earned him the appointment of General-in-Chief by President Abraham Lincoln in 1864. According to its regimental history, the Ninety-fifth Illinois Infantry fought in a long list of important conflicts, including the bloody Vicksburg campaign, which lasted from May until July 4, 1863. A Mississippi city known as "The Gibraltar of the Confederacy," Vicksburg was a major strategic stronghold located high on the bluffs guarding the Mississippi River. After a forty-seven-day siege of the city, Grant's army finally succeeded. The Confederate surrender at Vicksburg split the South, cutting off a major supply line for the Rebels, and the Union regained control of the river, which had been closed to navigation upon secession. The economic importance of regaining commercial access to the Mississippi River was imperative to the Union cause, and Lincoln made sure his civil and military leaders knew it: "See what a lot of land these fellows hold, of which Vicksburg is the key! The war can never be brought to a close until that key is in our pocket."

Though the victory reopened the Mississippi and helped raise Northern morale, the Vicksburg campaign in the spring of 1863 proved to be the most difficult time in the war for young Private Cashier, who reportedly was captured by Confederate soldiers while on a reconnaissance mission in the area. She managed to escape by forcing her way past the guard and fleeing back to the safety of Union camp. Later that summer, in June 1863, Jennie also suffered from chronic diarrhea, a chief killer of soldiers in the field (including fellow Union soldier-in-disguise Rosetta Wakeman), and was admitted to a military hospital. During the Vicksburg campaign, the rate of diarrhea and dysentery among the troops approached an appalling 50 percent. Soldiers and doctors alike were ignorant of many basic principles of microbial infection and sanitation, and one wartime surgeon noted that "men were in the habit of going out into the bushes, and not infrequently some 30 or 40 feet from some of their tents and relieving themselves"—often in direct range of drinking-water sources.

Though seriously ill, Jennie somehow "persuaded the hospital doctors to treat her for this highly debilitating illness as an outpatient, sparing her the embarrassment of discovery," notes Leonard in *All the Daring of the Soldier*. Like Rosetta Wakeman, Jennie was able to successfully avoid almost-certain detection while being cared for in the military hospital setting. It is true that the hospital system was virtually nonexistent at the start of the war, but by the time Jennie entered it in mid-1863, the U.S. Sanitary Commission was in existence. Both the Union and Confederate armies had begun constructing general hospitals—in clean, well-ventilated conditions—with greatly improved care for the sick and wounded. In this environment, for Jennie to carry on her charade undetected through her illness was a great feat, though it was generally noted by comrades that Private Cashier kept to himself—behavior that was not at all unusual for soldiers trying to cope with the continuing stress of war.

After her recovery, Jennie continued her military service with the Ninety-fifth Infantry Regiment. They participated in the Red River campaign, which ran from March 10 to May 22, 1864—pivotal because the Confederacy failed to win the series of battles decisively, in a way that might have changed the course of the war—as well as the battle of Guntown, Mississippi, on June 10, 1864, in which much of

the Ninety-fifth was wiped out. The rest of the regiment ended its
service the following year in the Gulf of Mexico near Mobile,
Alabama. After three years of rigorous service, including participation
in more than forty battles and engagements, Jennie Hodgers was hon-
orably discharged on August 17, 1865, when she mustered out at
Camp Butler, near Springfield, Illinois. According to its regimental
history in *Dyer's Compendium*, the Ninety-fifth Infantry Regiment lost
a total of 289 enlisted men and officers during the course of its service—205 of them to disease. Probably well aware of how close she had
come to joining the losses, Jennie Hodgers returned to Belvidere,
Illinois, and continued her life as Albert Cashier.

Jennie moved through several Illinois towns before settling in
Saunemin, a small village in Livingston County 75 miles southwest of
Chicago, in 1869. She continued to find work as a farmhand and a
handyman, as well as performing other odd jobs around the town.
Saunemin residents remembered her lighting the gas street lanterns
and stoking the church fire in the evenings, and town records show
Albert Cashier on the payroll for a few dollars a month. During the
course of her work, she became close with a successful local farming
family, the Chesebros, and lived in a one-room house built for her by
Joshua Chesebro. She came to spend much of her time with the family, even eating dinners with them at their home.

She seemed content with life in the small town, and other than her
relationship with the Chesebros, she maintained the social aloofness
that had served to protect her true identity throughout most of her
adult life. During the more than forty years that Jennie lived and
worked in Saunemin, she was intensely private and was often thought

of as eccentric. According to Peg Spalding's article "Union Maids," "Albert secured the door of his home with a number of locks, changing them frequently in case someone had obtained keys. If he were to be away overnight, Albert nailed the windows shut." Her guardedness, however, didn't prevent her from participating in other aspects of civic life. Though voting records were not kept until later, interviews with her neighbors and acquaintances around town corroborated that, as Albert Cashier, Jennie voted regularly at the polls.

According to records at the Illinois Soldiers' and Sailors' Home in which she later resided, Jennie's military pension was not granted until she was much older "for the reason that she would never submit to a physical examination on account of her secret." Her interview for a soldier's pension is dated on record as April 12, 1899. With the help of a friend and neighbor, Patrick Henry "P. H." Lannon, who filled out the form for her, she was able to answer the questionnaire—officially marking it with her "X" next to Lannon's own signature—and send it back to the Department of the Interior's Bureau of Pensions on April 20. In the pension interview, Jennie stated that she was never married and had no children. On a pension declaration dated March 11, 1907, Jennie proclaimed herself sixty-two years old. One of her document witnesses was former Illinois Senator Ira M. Lish, who occasionally employed Jennie for work around his house in Saunemin. She began receiving a pension of $8.00 a month, which was later increased to $12.00 according to various newspaper articles and her record at the soldiers' home, today the Illinois Veterans Home. Jennie also joined her beloved Grand Army of the Republic and participated in the local Decoration Day (the original Memorial Day, to commemorate those who died in the Civil War) parade each year. Elizabeth Leonard makes the important distinction that "unlike [Sarah Emma] Edmonds, Hodgers's membership in the G.A.R. was based on the continuing assumption that she was a man."

In 1910 Jennie became sick, and Mrs. Elizabeth Lannon sent a nurse to look in on her. The nurse was reported to have run back across the street and cried, "My Lord, Mrs. Lannon, he's a full-fledged woman!" Despite this finding, the two women kept the secret to themselves. But in 1911 the last wall against discovery was broken (along with her leg) when Jennie was hit by Senator Lish's car while doing maintenance work on his driveway. According to historian Elizabeth Leonard, Jennie was examined by Nettie Chesebro Rose, one of Joshua's daughters, though Peg Spalding notes that Senator Lish called on a Dr. C. F. Ross, who, during the course of his examination, also found Jennie to be a woman.

At first the Chesebros and Senator Lish kept Jennie's long-standing secret. But because Jennie was no longer able to work as she was accustomed, those caring for her eventually admitted her to the Illinois Soldiers' and Sailors' Home in May 1911, under the care of a Colonel Anderson (the commanding officer of the home mentioned in the Quincy *Whig* article). Here she was visited by several of the soldiers who had fought alongside her in the Ninety-fifth Regiment Infantry, including the former captain of her company. According to a 1928 letter from the Illinois Soldiers' and Sailors' Home, the captain had been living in Nebraska and called on Jennie at the home at least once: "The moment he saw her, he knew her and she knew him. At that time she was still in uniform, and was easy for him to make the recognition." At first Jennie's identity as a woman was kept secret by the administration at the soldiers' home, but she became increasingly unwell—subject to mental instability and erratic behavior—and was declared insane by the state of Illinois in 1913. In March of the following year, Jennie was transferred to the state Hospital for the Insane in Watertown, where she was forced to wear women's attire for the first time in more than fifty years.

Due to the unusual nature of the Albert Cashier–Jennie Hodgers case, the Federal Bureau of Pensions then began to request depositions from her fellow soldiers. The depositions were an attempt to determine if Jennie Hodgers was indeed the same person as the Albert Cashier who fought with the Illinois Ninety-fifth during the "War of the Rebellion." Jennie herself told inconsistent and conflicting stories about her past and thus could not be relied upon for testimony, though this could have been due to her habitual evasiveness concerning personal matters. As Leonard asks in *All the Daring of the Soldier*, "if Hodgers was truly mentally incapacitated by 1913, for example, might it not have been a result of the trauma of having her true identity exposed after so many years?" Was Illinois's insanity declaration in Jennie's case "even legitimate, given its timing in relation to the revelation that she was a woman?" In other words, was the insanity ruling the only way that the state knew how to deal with the phenomenon of having a female masquerade as one of its soldiers? A February 1915 Board of Review report even considered the far-fetched possibility that Jennie Hodgers was one of a pair of twins: "If such is the fact it is not improbable that the soldier actually was a man and that the pensioner is not the soldier."

All the regiment men included in her pension record gave agreeable impressions of their experiences with "the little soldier of the Ninety-fifth." Eventually the board agreed that Jennie Hodgers *was* Albert Cashier and continued to pay the pension until her death on October 10, 1915. (At the Department of the Interior's Pension Department, her last payment was noted on record at $25, after which her name was dropped from the pension roll for reason of death.) In a coffin draped with the American flag, Jennie Hodgers was dressed in her blue Union uniform and given an official Grand Army of the Republic funeral service, despite the fact that her gender had become common knowledge. Her body was buried with full military honors in Saunemin's Sunnyslope Cemetery in the Chesebro family plot. Two ministers performed the last rites under the G.A.R.'s Saunemin chapter.

Jennie left a small estate of about $500, largely composed of funds saved from her military pension. W. J. Singleton, the vice president of the Illinois State Bank of Quincy, was appointed administrator of her estate. He sent a December 2, 1915, letter to a Mary Rooney of Philadelphia, who had evidently contacted Captain J. E. Andrews at the Illinois Soldiers' and Sailors' Home inquiring about the inheritance. In his letter he described the funeral service as "wonderfully fine" and recapped the events of the previous few years, ending with a request that Mrs. Rooney and her brother "bring on your proof of your heirship and relationship to her [Jennie Hodgers] to the County Court of this [Livingston] county, who has jurisdiction over her estate." There is no apparent evidence that anything came of this request, but after a period of about eight years, an interesting correspondence began between John W. Reig, managing officer of the Illinois Soldiers' and

Sailors' Home, and one of Jennie's alleged nephews, Joseph Rooney of San Francisco.

"Her right name was Hodges or Hodgers and she was a half sister of my mother's," wrote Joseph in a letter dated January 5, 1924. "When she died she left some money in the Bank, and my brother in Ireland was notified, but this money was never received by any of us. The World War came along and my three sons and myself went to War, nevertheless we could not give this attention. . . . As we are home now and things are normal, I would like very much if you could furnish me the name of the Bank." He claimed to be the nearest of kin and was eager to settle the matter quickly. At least two more letters followed, on record at the Illinois Veterans Home. The last correspondence was dated November 24, 1924, and was written by Joseph Rooney's lawyer, Leo Rabinowitz. Because the administrator of the home could never establish that any of the claimants were authentic relatives of Jennie Hodgers—the case had been covered extensively in the print media, as shown by the newspaper clippings that several of the "heirs" sent along as "evidence"—the estate was closed. The Livingston County treasurer still holds the money today.

The name "Pvt. Albert D. J. Cashire" (this spelling came according to the Adjutant General of the State of Illinois) can be found on the interior wall of the Illinois Memorial in Vicksburg National Military Park. The original headstone still stands in Sunnyslope Cemetery, inscribed simply with the words "Albert D. J. Cashier, Co. G, 95 Ill. Inf." A new headstone was added by community groups in the late 1970s or early 1980s in an effort to identify who "Albert Cashier" really was and mark her proper place in history. Visitors to Saunemin today will see both the older marker and the larger memorial stone: "Albert D. J. Cashier, Co. G, 95 Ill. Inf. Civil War, born Jennie Hodgers in Clogher Head, Ireland, 1843–1915."

FRANCES CLAYTON, FLORENA BUDWIN,
MARY ANN CLARK, MARY PITMAN,
AND OTHER WOMEN SOLDIERS

"Some of the gentler sex who disguised themselves and swapped broomsticks for muskets were able to sustain the deception for amazingly long periods of time."

—*historian Bell Irvin Wiley,*
The Life of Billy Yank: The Common Soldier of the Union

OF THOSE WOMEN SOLDIERS who masqueraded as men, the paper trails left by Sarah Edmonds, Rosetta Wakeman, and Jennie Hodgers are by far the easiest to follow. Although it's likely that the precise number of female combatants will never be known, there are snippets—photos, newspapers, letters, and anecdotal evidence—that indicate the existence of many other interesting cases. DeAnne Blanton and Lauren M. Cook document three African-American female soldiers in *They Fought Like Demons*, though details are scant. Countless women, though they may not actually have joined the army to fight, shared the urge to become a soldier and expressed that sentiment in letters and diaries. "If I were only a man," wrote Sarah Morgan in her well-known Civil War diary. "Then I could don the breeches, and slay them with a will! If some Southern women were in the ranks, they could set the men an example they would not be blush to follow."

According to many accounts, Frances Clayton (also recorded as Francis Clalin) enlisted in 1861 with her husband, John, at St. Paul, Minnesota. They fought together for the Union in eighteen battles, until she was wounded and John was killed in the battle at Stones River in December 1862. Elizabeth Leonard writes that "Clayton was hospitalized with a bullet in her hip, and an examination led to the discovery of her sex and her eventual discharge." In a pamphlet used by famous women's suffragist Carrie Chapman Catt in her efforts to win women the vote, D. R. Livermore wrote this about Clayton: "She was wounded three times while fighting bravely for her country, and was once taken prisoner. Could not such a woman defend her vote?"

Two surviving photographs of Frances Clayton are held by the Trustees of the Boston Public Library. In one she is dressed as a woman, seated and wearing a long gown over a white blouse, her short brown hair carefully arranged in feminine fashion. In the other portrait she is equally convincing in a soldier's uniform, with her height and lean frame clearly working to her advantage. She was described in several newspaper articles as a tall, masculine-looking woman, proficient in the soldierly arts of drinking, smoking, chewing tobacco, and swearing.

Frances Clayton's story was the basis of Beth Gilleland's 1996 play *Civil Ceremony*, which premiered at the Great American History Theatre in Minneapolis. As reviewed by Michael Tortorello in the *City Pages*, even while they bore the weighty burden of war, women such as Frances Clayton found a valuable measure of freedom: "War, we learn, is dysentery and high piles of amputated limbs. Incomplete remains and shallow mass graves. . . . Yet, at the end of the play, Francis [sic] still describes these soldiering days as her best; even the constraints of

Frances Clayton (also Clalin) in soldier's uniform.

CREDIT: BOSTON PUBLIC LIBRARY/RARE BOOKS DEPARTMENT. COURTESY OF THE TRUSTEES

gender subterfuge are looser binds than those of the Victorian corset." But Tortorello also points out that the achievement is a short-lived one. Despite Frances Clayton's success in the masquerade, "women had progressed as far as they would in the military for another century."

Oblivious to the lengthy struggle for equality in the armed services that would follow, soldier women such as Frances Clayton acted with more immediate results in mind. Twenty-two-year-old Frances Hook, alias Frank Miller, was believed to have joined the Sixty-fifth Illinois Home Guard early in the war to be with her brother. The two enlisted for a term of three months and then moved on to join the Ninetieth Illinois Infantry. Her brother was killed at the Battle of Shiloh, but, with no family to return to, Frances continued to fight. She was captured by Confederate forces near Florence, Alabama, in 1864 and shot in the leg while attempting to escape.

In June 1864 the Chelsea *Telegraph and Pioneer* reported that "rebels searched her person for papers, discovered her sex, respected her as a women, and gave her a sperate [sic] room while in prison at Atlanta, Ga." The newspaper also claimed that Confederate President Jefferson Davis wrote Frances a letter offering a lieutenant's commission if she joined their ranks, but she refused to accept such a commission from the Rebel army. "The insurgents tried to exhort from her a promise that she would go home and not enter the service again. 'Go home!' she said: 'My only brother was killed at Pittsburg Landing, and I have no home—no friends!'" She was subsequently traded in a prisoner exchange and moved to a Union general hospital in Chattanooga. During this time Frances Hook encountered Dr. Mary Walker, who "described Frank as of about medium hight [sic], with dark hazel eyes, dark brown hair, rounded features and feminine voice and appearance."

A May 1934 New York *Times* article told the story of Florena (or Florina) Budwin, who enlisted together with her husband in the Union army. Both soldiers were captured and incarcerated at Andersonville, the Confederate prison notorious for its horrendously unsanitary conditions. Florena survived her husband there long enough to be moved to another Confederate prison in Florence, South Carolina. Health conditions were not much different in the Florence facility, however, and she became sick and was at last identified as a woman by a prison doctor. "Dr. Josephus Hall must have been a conscientious or an observant physician," write Blanton and Cook in *They Fought Like Demons*. "It was he who finally recognized that Budwin was a woman." Florena immediately received her own room and better treatment, but as Blanton and Cook reveal in their detailed military history, which documents about 250 women who saw combat, "she died of pneumonia on January 25, 1865, only one month before all the sick prisoners at Florence were paroled and sent north. She was 20 years old." Today Florena Budwin's grave is marked at the National Cemetery in Florence, where she is buried alongside other Union prisoners of war who died at the prison.

Another woman who enlisted with a loved one was Frances Day, who served briefly as Sergeant Frank Mayne with the 126th Pennsylvania Infantry to be with William Fitzpatrick. After William's death from illness just shortly after enlistment, a grief-stricken Frances became a deserter. According to William F. Fox's *Regimental Losses in the American Civil War 1861–1865*, "Mayne is listed as having deserted on August 24, 1862; but was subsequently killed in battle in another regiment where it was discovered that she was a woman."

There are myriad similar stories: Mary Siezgle originally joined the Union army as a nurse but became a soldier like her husband in the Forty-fourth New York Infantry. Lizzie Compton was shown to be a woman after being wounded in battle and claimed service to seven different regiments because of repeated discovery. Mary Owens, who was profiled in a 1901 article in the New York *Sun*, was discovered after being wounded for a third time while in battle with her Pennsylvania regiment. The First Kentucky Infantry's Private John Thompson was revealed when she attracted attention with her feminine way of putting on stockings, as Albert Richardson detailed in *The Secret Service, the Field, the Dungeon, and the Escape*.

Because the Confederacy was not as copious in its documentation as the Union was, fewer records of Confederate women soldiers have survived. Some of the female fighters show up anonymously in letters, such as one by Union soldier Thomas Reed, who wrote to his parents in August 1863 about a Confederate woman wounded at Gettysburg, cited in *They Fought Like Demons:* "I must tel [sic] you we have got a female secesh here. She was wounded at gettysburg but our doctors soon found her out . . . the poor girl [h]as lost a leg." Several other Confederate women served as soldiers: Mary Ann Clark, according to Blanton and Cook, fought with General Braxton Bragg in the Tennessee theater in 1862 and eventually became a lieutenant. She was wounded in the leg at the Battle of Richmond, Kentucky, and became a Union POW. A member of a Virginia artillery regiment, Sarah Jane Ann Perkins fought for the Confederacy from the war's beginning and was captured by the Union at Hanover Junction. Charlotte Hope (alias Charlie Hopper) fought for the Confederacy in the First Virginia Cavalry and "appeared to her comrades to be a boy about sixteen years of age," according to *They Fought Like Demons*. Blanton and Cook document the case of Ellen Levasay, a member of the Third Missouri Cavalry, who turned herself in to Union forces at Vicksburg and was imprisoned for about eight months in Camp Morton, Indiana. By the spring of 1864, "Levasay obviously could not stand being a prisoner any longer . . . [that April] she took the oath of allegiance to the United States and was liberated."

One unusual case, Mary Pitman, aka Lieutenant Rawley, served both the Confederacy and the Union at different points during the war. As a Confederate soldier, she led an independent cavalry company from Tennessee at the Battle of Shiloh and later revealed her true identity to Confederate General Nathan Bedford Forrest so that she could work as a female spy for the South. But she eventually defected to the Union, where her knowledge of Southern plots was valuable to her work as a Federal spy. In January 1865, writes Leonard in *All the Daring of the Soldier*, "the Union's Provost Marshal General of Missouri, J. H. Baker, issued a pass to one Mary M. Pitman . . ." Government records indicate that she was dispatched on confidential missions and, what's more, paid well for her services. "With the exception of Malinda Blalock," who soldiered for just a month with the Confederacy before "engag[ing] in pro-Union bushwhacking" in North Carolina and Tennessee, Blanton and Cook hold that Mary Pitman is the only female soldier who did not stay loyal to her side throughout the Civil War.

"Daughters of the Regiment"

> "It was not strange, years later . . . that the recollections of the camp fire in front of her father's tent, as well as the devotion of a newly-married wife, and loyalty to the Union, prompted her to follow her husband, stand beside him in battle, and share all his hardships."
>
> —*Frank Moore, "The Heroine of Newbern,"* Women of the War

IN FRANK MOORE'S 1866 book *Women of the War,* a teenage girl named Kady Brownell played a starring role. Born in 1842 on the African coast, Kady (maiden name Southwell) was "accustomed to arms and soldiers from infancy"—her father was a Scottish soldier in the British army stationed there. According to Moore, "she learned to love the camp," and those childhood experiences laid the groundwork for her later adventures on the Civil War battlefield. It's unclear how much of her story was embellished as Moore told it, but much of Kady's early life is substantiated and documented in Elizabeth Leonard's *All the Daring of the Soldier.* After the death of her mother, Kady moved to the United States to live with the McKinzies, who, according to Leonard, were family friends. Kady eventually found work as a weaver, and in March 1861 she married Robert S. Brownell in Providence, Rhode Island.

The first shots were fired at Fort Sumter not long after, on April 12, 1861, and the first Union enlistees followed, among them Robert Brownell. Rather than remain at home, Kady accompanied her husband into battle with the First Rhode Island Infantry Volunteers in the summer of 1861. She was nineteen years old. Eventually she was made the color-bearer of the First Rhode Island's eleventh company of sharpshooters.

Kady's efforts to follow her husband into camp are described in detail by Elizabeth Leonard. Ambrose E. Burnside—who would later become the commander of the Army of the Potomac during one of its worst defeats (the battle of Fredericksburg) and three-time governor of Rhode Island, and whose major legacy is the term "sideburns" due to his unique cut of facial hair—was at the time the colonel of the First Rhode Island. Burnside "turned her back" when she "revealed her intention to remain with her husband." But Kady managed to gain Rhode Island Governor William Sprague's approval to stay with the regiment. Leonard cites a February 16, 1913, New York *Times* article that described the four women who tenaciously hung on and followed the regiment into camp: "'a laundress and three [soldiers'] relatives' who had 'utterly refused to be left at home' "—one of whom was reported to be Kady Brownell. Of these army women, Kady was adopted as the "daughter of the regiment."

A woman who took on this role was meant to be an attractive and inspiring figure to the soldiers—even a kind of "mascot or 'guardian angel,' " says Leonard. At times the daughter of the regiment was

A portrait of vivandière Kady Brownell in army costume.

CREDIT: LIBRARY OF CONGRESS, LC–USZ62-110631

literally a daughter (or wife) of a regimental officer. Primary duties included work as a nurse, to give medical attention to the troops on and off the battlefield. Daughters of the regiment were part of a tradition of army women that had its roots in Europe. During the nineteenth century the French army under Napoleon made official the residence of a few women they called *vivandières*. Like camp sutlers, vivandières at that time primarily sold food and drink to the soldiers, but they also acted to boost morale. The French army established the vivandière role to reduce the number of female camp followers, some of whom were prostitutes. To distinguish their role in the army, vivandières began wearing clothing similar to the men they worked beside, albeit more ornate: fancier hats and skirts worn over long trousers. In the process the vivandière uniform gradually became militarized, and eventually the women carried arms of their own, including short swords and pistols.

Leonard writes that "for centuries European women had effectively created a variety of positions for themselves—some even paramilitary in nature—within the military systems." The presence of women during the American Revolution is evidence that the tradition was carried over the Atlantic. Female relatives of Continental Army soldiers were paid to cook, nurse, and otherwise provide for the troops. The fact that they were also subject to military discipline indicates that their role was as formalized and integral to the army as that of a male soldier. For example, Leonard notes that certain women were assigned duty to bring water to gun crews and probably "moved . . . to actually loading and firing army weapons themselves when the situation demanded it"—i.e., when male comrades were shot or otherwise incapacitated in the line of fire.

During the Civil War, women like Kady Brownell also took on more than symbolic posts in their regiment. According to the U.S. Army Military History Institute, Civil War vivandières eventually transcended the narrow dictionary definition of female sutler to include "laundresses, prostitutes, female combatants, and other camp followers, including wives of enlisted men and noncommissioned officers." The institute notes that because of this, "the number of actual vivandières present in Union and Confederate armies depends upon the interpretation of the term." Vivandières could also be loosely described as "women who followed the army in a quasi-military capacity," writes Susan Lyons Hughes in her article "The Daughter of the Regiment: A Brief History of Vivandières and Cantinieres in the American Civil War." Hughes points out that what distinguished vivandières from the likes of Sarah Emma Edmonds and Sarah Rosetta Wakeman was that the former "made no effort to disguise their sex." They performed all their appointed duties—bearing the colors on the battlefield and during troop movements from one military theater to the next, rallying the soldiers with the flag when they lost morale in battle, nursing soldiers while braving the front lines, sometimes amid a hail of enemy bullets, even participating in the firing themselves—as women. As Leonard puts it, "The battlefield was indeed a place where individual roles and tasks became less distinct, and all available personnel, regardless of sex, were known to take up arms on occasion."

In *Women of the War*, Moore was among the first writers to forge a place for Kady Brownell in history. In her official role as daughter of the regiment, he wrote, she was not a "mere water-carrier," "ornamental appendage," or "graceful figure on parade," but proved herself to be "effective against the enemy" on the field of battle. She practiced handling arms daily, drilling with the First Rhode Island when they were stationed in camp in Maryland. She was said to be "one of the quickest and most accurate marksmen in the regiment," as well as proficient with the straight sword she carried in her belt. At first Kady acted as a color-bearer on the field, carrying and protecting the flag, which served as a rallying point for the regiment. In mid-July 1861 she marched with her company south toward the Confederate capital of Richmond and is said to have held her regiment's flag high at the First Battle of Bull Run. During her service with the First Rhode Island, a photograph was taken that depicts her in her battle dress, with a knee-length skirt over pants, a sash at her waist, and a sword in her hand.

When the First Rhode Island disbanded in August 1861—its soldiers had just a three-month term—both Brownells reenlisted in the Fifth Rhode Island Infantry two months later. Once again, Kady was the color-bearer of the regiment, but she also worked as a nurse. At the battle of New Bern, North Carolina, on March 14, 1862, Kady's quick action on the field saved her regiment from "friendly fire." According to Moore, the Fifth Rhode Island was at first mistaken for a Rebel force and was on the verge of being fired upon when Kady ran out to the front lines, waving the Union flag until "it was apparent that the advancing force were friends." Because of Kady's courageous appearance on the battlefield in New Bern, Moore dubbed her "The Heroine of Newbern."

During the battle Kady ministered to several wounded soldiers, both Rebel and Union, including her husband, Robert, who was shot in the leg with a minié ball. The Union army was triumphant that day,

An unidentified vivandière wearing infantry hat and cape.
CREDIT: THE GILDER LEHRMAN COLLECTION, COURTESY OF THE GILDER LEHRMAN
INSTITUTE OF AMERICAN HISTORY, NEW YORK

eventually capturing and occupying New Bern. A 1913 New York *Times* article quotes Kady as saying, "That fight was short, sharp, and sweet. . . . I was in it from beginning to end until my husband got the rifle ball which crippled him." She added that the risk of making herself vulnerable at the front lines was "necessary, you see, to inspire the men. Whenever they saw me they rallied around me. I felt that the sight of a woman might inspire them, and I think it did." Some postwar doubts were raised about the exact details of her battle accomplishments, but she also had a host of supporters—enough to garner her a government pension later in life. Leonard presents the testimonies of various officers who witnessed the battle of New Bern, describing several former captains who asserted that they were "unaware that she [Kady] had done anything particularly brave during the battle," though they acknowledged that she had very attentively and conscientiously tended to the wounded. Despite these lukewarm accounts, the story of Kady Brownell inspired many a literary tribute in the form of poetry, newspaper articles, and books.

In the weeks following the battle, Kady stayed in New Bern with Robert and helped nurse him back to health. In April 1862 the two boarded a steamship to New York, where Robert recuperated at the Soldier's Relief Hospital. It was "eighteen months before he touched ground, and then the surgeons pronounced him unfit for active service; and as his soldier days were over," Moore proclaimed in *Women of the War*, "Kady had no thought of anything more" than fulfilling the role of "loving wife." Both Brownells eventually set up a new home in New York and were released from military service.

According to Moore, Kady kept the flag she carried in battle, as well as her discharge papers, "signed A. E. Burnside, and the sergeant sword, with her name cut on the scabbard." Because the Brownells found it difficult to stay afloat financially, in 1884 Kady applied for and received a government pension of $8.00 a month. (According to Leonard, Robert received $24 a month.) She worked as an employee of the New York City Department of Parks for ten years before becoming a custodian in the Washington Heights neighborhood of upper Manhattan. She would continue to live with her husband in New York until her death on January 5, 1915, at the Woman's Relief Corps Home in Oxford, New York. She was seventy-two.

Though a prominent vivandière and daughter of the regiment, Kady Brownell was only one of several known examples of what Leonard calls "half-soldier heroines," women whose capacity in the army anticipated the changing gender roles of the day. They functioned as nurses and as lofty symbols of a feminine ideal, but due to necessity their purpose also moved beyond those safe confines into the traditionally male arena of battle. Perhaps the most celebrated of all was Anna "Annie" Etheridge. She may have followed her husband when he joined the Second Michigan at the beginning of the war, but she did not follow his example when he deserted soon afterward. After serving as the daughter of the Third Michigan's regiment, she continued her service with the Fifth Michigan until war's end.

Reported to have carried two pistols for her protection while she worked, Annie was famed for taking her horse to the front of battle to tend to those hurt in the front lines, her saddlebags full of medical supplies. On horseback she also rallied the troops during lulls in the action. She also cooked in camp and shared the same conditions as male soldiers, insisting on sleeping on the ground with just a blanket. After four years with the Union army, Annie was an experienced and well-regarded "veteran of a number of the war's most gruesome engagements and campaigns," according to Leonard. Sources place her at both the First and Second Battles of Bull Run and the battles of

A photograph of Annie Etheridge.
CREDIT: STATE ARCHIVES OF MICHIGAN

Williamsburg, Antietam, Fredericksburg, and Gettysburg, among others. Through the trials of those battles, she became known as a tireless and kind presence on the field, "always on hand and ready to bear the same privations as the men," in the words of one soldier in 1863. Indeed, Annie Etheridge appeared in the letters and journals of many soldiers throughout the war. She was described as unflinching in the face of danger—even amid exploding shells that shredded her clothing as she dressed the wounds of the injured.

War nurses such as Mary Livermore and Cornelia Hancock spoke highly of this well-respected daughter of the regiment. In a March 1865 letter home, Cornelia wrote of Etheridge's dedicated work at a fixed army hospital, where she had a stint as a result of General Ulysses S. Grant's fall 1864 order to remove all women from camps in his military theater of operations: "Annie Etheridge is now ordered from the front to stay at the hospt. (City Point) and is very bare of clothing." Various officers she worked with petitioned General Grant to have Annie stay on duty with them. Although the petition failed, it spoke of the value of her contributions.

Annie Etheridge wasn't the only vivandière remembered for her courageous efforts in battle. For their valor, she and a French-born vivandière named Marie Tepe were both awarded the Kearny Cross on May 16, 1863, after the battle of Chancellorsville. The Kearny Cross, established just two months earlier to honor noncommissioned officers and privates who had distinguished themselves in battle, was named for Major General Philip Kearny, who was killed in Virginia at the battle of Chantilly on September 1, 1862. Etheridge and Tepe were the only two women to receive the medals out of more than 300 awarded. Known as "French Mary," Marie Tepe was in service with the 27th and 114th Pennsylvania Infantry Regiments and was reportedly wounded in the ankle at the battle of Fredericksburg.

Annie Etheridge mustered out of service with her regiment in July 1865. Her petition for a pension was approved by Congress in February 1887, for an amount of $25 per month. After her death on January 23, 1913, at Georgetown University Hospital, Annie Etheridge was buried in Arlington National Cemetery.

Other notable women who played the role of regiment daughter included Bridget Divers, who was also known as Bridget Deavers and Bridget Devins, an Irish immigrant who rode with the First Michigan Cavalry in their raids and was famous for rallying the troops with her enthusiasm and expert horsemanship. She is reported to have stayed with the army after the war was over to help defend the western frontier. And although there are no specific mentions of her engagement in "military or paramiltary activities per se," according to Leonard, Arabella "Belle" Reynolds was famed for her skills as a nurse and dogged determination as daughter of the Seventeenth Illinois Infantry. She was particularly honored for her actions at the bloody battle of Shiloh in April 1862, where she cared for the hundreds wounded in that battle. She also brandished a revolver to prevent desperately retreating soldiers from overrunning the hospital ship *Emerald,* docked at Pittsburg Landing. "For thirty-six hours we found no rest," she wrote of the tumultuous events. Her experience there garnered her the honorary rank of major from Governor Richard Yates of Illinois. (See the "Wartime Nurses" chapter for a more thorough examination of her accomplishments as a nurse.)

These are among the best known of those women who acted in a quasi-military capacity as vivandières or daughters of the regiment, officially and unofficially, during the Civil War. Numerous others were mentioned in newspaper reports during and after the war, including Sarah (Sallie) Taylor, Nadine Turchin, Hannah Ewbank, and Southerner Lucy Ann Cox, who served with the Thirteenth Virginia until Confederate General Robert E. Lee's surrender to Union General Ulysses S. Grant at Appomattox Court House. What's known about many of these women's military careers is limited to the bits culled from newspapers, diaries, and letters from the war. Occasionally military records of their service have provided valuable documentary evidence, but, as many acted unofficially in the war, such records are few and far between.

Spies

ROSE O'NEAL GREENHOW, BELLE BOYD, PAULINE CUSHMAN,

ELIZABETH VAN LEW, AND HARRIET TUBMAN

"The secret chamber in which Miss Lizzie Van Lew concealed in her home the Federal prisoners whom she helped to escape from Libby Prison during the war has just been located in the old Van Lew mansion, at Richmond, Va. It is an attic room, under the roof, five feet in pitch at the highest point and as dark as a prison cell. . . . It is not believed that Miss Van Lew ever showed the room to anybody."

—from the National Tribune, *November 15, 1900*

OFF THE BATTLEFIELD and in the drawing room, a number of intrepid women made contributions of a different nature during the Civil War—as spies. Although they seemed to be working in their normal daily capacity, these women in fact stretched the confines of their traditional roles—as social hostesses, actresses, nurses, and slaves—to help their respective causes. The knowledge they garnered while in conventional realms often could be used tactically against the enemy. For example, Confederate spy Antonia Ford was instrumental in the capture of Union General Edwin H. Stoughton in March 1863, which was a disgrace to the North. Commissioned by Confederate General J. E. B. Stuart on what may have been a lark, Antonia nevertheless gathered intelligence through seemingly innocent social interactions with Union soldiers in Fairfax Court House, Virginia, and transmitted it to Confederate authorities. The most well-known women spies included Rose O'Neal Greenhow, Belle Boyd, Pauline Cushman, Elizabeth Van Lew, and Harriet Tubman. Their stories offer an interesting cross section of those who broke from gender convention and fought the Civil War in a different way.

Rose O'Neal Greenhow, nicknamed "Wild Rose" and "Rebel Rose," was one of the most celebrated Confederate spies in the Civil War. She was born in 1817 into a wealthy family in Montgomery County, Maryland. She became an ardent secessionist and a significant hostess in Washington society, often mingling with such influential politicians as her good friend John C. Calhoun (the South Carolina statesman famous for his doctrine of states' rights) and James Buchanan (U.S. president before Lincoln, he was unable to mediate a widening sectional rift). She was passionate about preserving the Southern way of life and intensely loyal to its interests, slavery included.

Married to Dr. Robert Greenhow and the mother of four daughters, Rose was a forty-four-year-old widow by the time war broke out in 1861. She became more and more involved in advocating the Southern cause and, through her charms and her many contacts in Washington, organized an espionage ring. Her major accomplishment was the communication of Union troop movements to Confederate General Pierre G. T. Beauregard just prior to the First Battle of Bull Run in July 1861. She had the message ciphered, sewn up in a tiny silk package, and hidden in the hair of a courier named Betty Duvall, who rode out to the Fairfax County courthouse from Washington dressed as a simple country girl. The message found its way to Beauregard, who was then able to amass enough troops before the battle to obtain a victory. General Beauregard and Confederate President Jefferson Davis both credited Rose with contributing significantly to the Union defeat at Bull Run, although some historians question the actual impact of her communiqué, as Beauregard undoubtedly had other sources working in his favor.

The fledgling United States Secret Service, headed by detective Allan Pinkerton, became increasingly suspicious of Rose Greenhow. A search of her home on August 23, 1861, found incriminating maps and documents, and she was arrested and confined there. The house became known as "Fort Greenhow," but even in captivity Rose was still able to transmit secret information to the Confederacy.

A special archival collection at Duke University is devoted to Rose Greenhow's papers, which include correspondence that dealt with her spy activities for the South. On November 17, 1861, Rose wrote a letter to Secretary of State William H. Seward describing her imprisonment and protesting the state of government: "For nearly three months I have been confined, a close prisoner, shut out from air and exercise, and denied all communication with family and friends. . . . The 'iron heel of power' may keep down, but it cannot crush out, the spirit of resistance in a people armed for the defence of their rights; and I tell you now, sir, that you are standing over a crater, whose smothered fires in a moment may burst forth." A copy of the zealous note found its way to the Richmond *Whig*, where it was published for propaganda

A portrait of Rose Greenhow and her daughter at the Old Capitol Prison,
taken by Mathew Brady's studio photographer, Alexander Gardner.
CREDIT: LIBRARY OF CONGRESS, LC-USZ62-3131

purposes. The newspaper called it the "most graphic sketch yet given to the world" of the "cruel and dastardly tyranny" of the Yankee government and noted that this important record of "the incarceration and torture of helpless women, and the outrages heaped upon them" was bound to "shock" many in the audience, who would then "stamp the Lincoln dynasty everywhere with undying infamy."

For about three months, Rose was kept under house arrest in Fort Greenhow, along with several other "secession women" who acted against the U.S. government. In an article dated November 29, 1861 (source unknown), the house is described as an "ordinary" three-story brick building, with "uncommonly dirty" windows and a "lazy sentinel" spotted gossiping with his friend. The female prisoners were held on the house's second floor, and Rose was outraged that lower-class women "of bad character"—as she wrote to Secretary Seward—were placed in her own house with her.

Because Rose was persistent in her espionage activities from Fort Greenhow, she and her eight-year-old daughter, "Little Rose," were transferred to Washington, D.C.'s, Old Capitol Prison the following January 1862. Even from this location, however, Rose was somehow able to continue her covert communications. Renowned Civil War photographer Mathew Brady had a portrait of Rose and her daughter taken by Alexander Gardner, one of his studio photographers, during their confinement at the Old Capitol. In a bare dirty room under a shuttered window, Rose remains the picture of Southern refinement— and defiance—while wearing a black dress and holding her daughter close. The photograph was published as part of Mathew Brady's series *Incidents of War,* and the albumen silver print is now a part of the National Portrait Gallery's collection at the Smithsonian Institution in Washington, D.C.

In his Washington *Post* article " 'Rebel Rose,' A Spy of Grande Dame Proportions," Michael Farquhar writes that it was this imprisonment, this dramatic sacrificial role, that was Rose Greenhow's "greatest service to the South . . . far more than the information she secretly provided." Farquhar quotes Princeton University historian James McPherson on the impact that Rose had upon Confederate morale: "They made her a martyr in the eyes of the Southern people . . . The brutal Yankees who would imprison a mother and child provided ammunition for the Confederate propaganda mills."

After a judicial hearing that charged her with espionage, Rose was exiled to the South for the remainder of the war. She was brought out of the Federal capital of Washington draped in the Confederate flag, and when she arrived in the Confederate capital of Richmond, she was welcomed with open arms as a heroine of the Southern cause.

But her work wasn't yet finished. Soon after her release she traveled abroad to Britain and France as a one-woman propaganda machine, using her powers of persuasion to raise support and sympathy for the South. Rose successfully gained audiences with Queen Victoria and Napoleon III and circulated widely in upper-class social circles. During 1863, her year abroad, she also published a best-selling book of writings in London entitled *My Imprisonment and the First Year of Abolition Rule at Washington.* She dedicated the work to "the brave soldiers who have fought and bled in this our glorious struggle for freedom." In the book Rose detailed her objections to the Lincoln administration—calling his election "an Invasion of Southern Rights"—and her "humiliating" imprisonment in Washington. Her account is a valuable record of the predominant Southern sentiments that led up to the Civil War, the indignation and feelings of dishonor that continued through the conflict as Confederates witnessed what they saw as unfair Northern aggression, and the currents that would eventually influence postbellum events.

As she noted in the introduction to her book, Rose O'Neal Greenhow had "peculiar and exceptional means" of watching the conflict unfold: her intimate relations with important political figures in Washington society. Her role as a popular hostess, and a trusted one at that, enabled her to secure valuable information that later became useful to the Confederate states. As a woman well positioned in the social epicenter of the nation's capital, Rose Greenhow was able to use her intelligence, charm, and cunning to undermine the Union position in the conflict. Even captured and confined, Rose found ways to subvert her captors and use her imprisonment to drum up further support for the South. She showed that even through traditional channels, women could not be underestimated as effective instruments of war.

Because she *was* reared in the proper Southern tradition, however, she could not help but include a passage to mitigate her behavior and language, which "in ordinary times, and upon ordinary subjects," might not be perceived as "becoming in the personal narrative of a woman." She asked readers to "imagine themselves in my position—subject to the stinging indignities of a Washington prison . . . vicious taunts of vulgar guards . . . a little daughter, too, always before my eyes, torn from the peaceful delights of home, and the flowery path of girlhood, and forced to witness the hard realities of prison-life . . ." But perhaps this could also be seen as a calculated move on her part to win over the sympathy of those who might have seen her actions as too outrageous for the times.

In any case, Rose Greenhow's influence was wide and phenomenal. In 1864 she left Europe aboard the *Condor*, a British blockade-running ship bound for home. The ship ran aground in North Carolina at the mouth of the Cape Fear River, and she persuaded the captain to let her head for shore in a small rowboat. As she attempted to escape the Union gunboat that followed the *Condor*, Rose's boat capsized and she drowned. On October 1 the Wilmington Soldiers' Aid Society held a funeral for Rose O'Neal Greenhow with full military honors. Her coffin was covered with a Confederate flag and borne by Confederate soldiers to the town's Oakdale Cemetery. A newspaper clipping from the Wilmington *Sentinel* detailing the event noted that it was a "solemn and imposing spectacle . . . the tide of visitors, women and children with streaming eyes, and soldiers, with bent heads and hushed stares, standing by, paying the last tribute of respect to the departed heroine." The marble cross marking her grave is inscribed with the words "Mrs. Rose O'N. Greenhow, a bearer of dispatchs [sic] to the Confederate Government."

Another renowned Confederate spy was the flamboyant Belle Boyd, who grew up in Martinsburg, Virginia (now part of West Virginia), as the daughter of a farmer and merchant. Born in 1844, she debuted in Washington society at the war's inception—the winter of 1860–1861— and eventually became famous as a Confederate informant for General Stonewall Jackson when she provided key details of Union army movements in the Shenandoah Valley area during spring 1862. The information led to Jackson's surprise attack and capture of Front Royal, Virginia. In return for her help, Jackson made Belle a captain and an honorary aide-de-camp. Belle also claimed to have shot a Union soldier who insulted her mother at the outset of war and took responsibility for smuggling quinine and acting as a courier of intelligence for the Confederacy in the tricky border area between the North and South.

Belle was arrested several times and imprisoned twice on charges of espionage: the first on July 29, 1862, when she was held for a month in the Old Capitol Prison in Washington, D.C., and eventually released on a prisoner exchange; the second in June 1863 at Carroll Prison, when she became ill with typhoid fever and was eventually released. She went to Britain in March 1864 bearing Confederate dispatches but was captured by a Union blockade warship and banished to Canada. During the incident she fell in love with Lieutenant Samuel Wylde Hardinge, the Union officer who took command of the Rebel ship. Belle made her way to England, where the lovers reunited and married on August 25, 1864, in St. James Church, Piccadilly. Samuel Hardinge was arrested by military authorities upon his return to the United States in December 1864 and was ultimately dismissed from the Navy for his mishandling of Belle's capture. From the Brunswick Hotel in London, Belle wrote a January 24, 1865, letter to President Lincoln in the hopes that he would have her husband released: "I have heard from good authority that if I suppress the Book I have now ready for publication, you may be induced to consider leniently the case of my husband, S. Wylde Hardinge, now a prisoner in Fort Delaware, I think it would be well for you & me to come to some definite understanding . . ."

No response was received from Lincoln, but Samuel was released from Fort Delaware in February, and he journeyed again to England. Belle's book, *Belle Boyd in Camp and Prison,* an at times ridiculously embellished version of her exploits as a spy in the American Civil War, was published later that year. She claimed that it was "not originally intended to be more than a personal narrative," but for various reasons

A photograph of Confederate spy Belle Boyd.

CREDIT: VIRGINIA HISTORICAL SOCIETY, RICHMOND, VA

the book became "political." Belle asserted that she wished to "open the eyes of Europe to many things of which the world on this side of the water little dreams."

Belle Boyd in Camp and Prison was written in two volumes and features a dashing portrait of her in dress gown, with what appears to be a white glove in one hand and a riding crop in the other, perhaps symbolic of her deep ties to the South. The account also had a somewhat overblown and flowery introduction by a "Friend of the South," who sang Belle's praises and compared the "young heroine" to Joan of Arc. The story was sold as an account of her "adventures, misfortunes, imprisonments, and persecutions," which she wrote "all from memory" during her time in London. Through the book, "La Belle Rebelle"—as many in the foreign press called her—made an unabashed plea for money. With her husband "in irons" at Fort Delaware and her father, a "most respectable Virginia gentleman," recently passed away, she claimed to be "destitute." In the second volume Belle turned the narrative over to her husband, who wrote of his own prison trials.

Belle Boyd and Samuel Hardinge had one daughter. After his death in 1866, Belle became an actress to support her child. Over the next twenty years she continued to appear on stage in Confederate uniform, lecturing to crowded theaters about her colorful and dramatic life as a spy. She married twice more and had four sons. The "Siren of the Shenandoah" died in Wisconsin on June 11, 1900, while on tour.

Another actress, Pauline Cushman, used her talent to aid the North. She was born on June 10, 1833, in New Orleans and made her most important stage entrance in 1862 while appearing in a play at a Louisville, Kentucky, theater—at the time, the city was under firm

Actress-turned-Union spy Pauline Cushman in soldier's uniform.
CREDIT: COURTESY OF THE GILDER LEHRMAN INSTITUTE OF AMERICAN HISTORY, NEW YORK

Union control. Before one evening's performance, she was dared by two Confederate officers to toast Confederate President Jefferson Davis. She did so, but not before reporting the proposition to a federal provost marshal. The incident got her fired from the theater company but established her "loyalties" and set Pauline up perfectly as a spy for the Union.

In the article "Acting Her Part: Narratives of Union Women Spies," author Lyde Cullen Sizer states that "as much as spying itself, spy stories, fictional or factual, offered women an important avenue for revising or directly challenging gender convention." She cites Pauline Cushman's 1864 pamphlet, *The Romance of the Great Rebellion,* in which Pauline describes herself as a woman whose "patriotism and nerve might be well employed as a 'detective' in the secret army service." That evening, Pauline wrote, she "never succeeded so well in any fictitious part as in this piece of serio-comic stage effect . . . to render the Government essential service." In her act she convinced the Confederates of her devotion to the Southern cause and was then able to serve the Union through her new role.

She became a camp follower, traveling with Confederate troops through Kentucky and Tennessee, using her feminine appeal to gather secret information and reporting military movements back to her Union contacts. Unfortunately, she was caught with sensitive documents while spying in Shelbyville. Confederate General Braxton Bragg, commander of the Army of Tennessee, had Pauline tried in a military court, which sentenced her to hang. She was saved from imminent death by the arrival of Union troops—General Bragg was forced to leave her behind as his army fled—and returned north to an enthusiastic reception. President Abraham Lincoln gave her an honorary commission as a major, and after the Civil War ended, Pauline Cushman combined both of her life careers on a tour in which she celebrated her wartime adventures as a spy. She gave lectures dressed in uniform and even performed for a time with famous showman P. T. Barnum. She also published a somewhat exaggerated biographical account in 1865, *The Life of Pauline Cushman,* written by her friend Ferdinand Sarmiento.

A full-length portrait photograph of Pauline Cushman can be viewed in the Pierpont Morgan Library's Gilder Lehrman collection. Standing with one arm resting on a podium covered with a printed blanket, she is outfitted in full dress uniform with sword against a battlefield backdrop with tents and an American flag. The exact date of the photograph, an albumen *carte de visite,* is unclear, but it was included in an album that was put together during the 1860s. Printed in verso: "Net proceeds from sales of these Photographs will be devoted to the education of Colored People in the deportment of the Gulf, now under the commend of Maj. Gen. Banks." Pauline was also photographed by Mathew Brady and by photographer Charles DeForest Fredricks, who shot her in a revealing theater costume circa 1866.

The cause of Pauline Cushman's death, on December 2, 1893, reflected her lifetime propensity for drama: a suicidal overdose of opium, which she had been taking for an illness. She was buried with military honors by the Grand Army of the Republic in San Francisco and rests today in the Officers' Section of the San Francisco National Cemetery in the Presidio.

Not all Civil War spies were quite so theatrical or brazen with their affairs. Elizabeth Van Lew was an incredibly effective spy for the North precisely because of her discretion. She was born into the Richmond, Virginia, merchant class on October 12, 1818. Her father, John Van Lew, was a successful hardware businessman originally from New York; her grandfather, Hilary Baker, was a mayor of Philadelphia.

Staunch Unionist, abolitionist, and Northern spy Elizabeth Van Lew.

CREDIT: VIRGINIA HISTORICAL SOCIETY, RICHMOND, VA

Though she was born in the South, she was schooled in Philadelphia and grew to become a staunch Unionist and fervent abolitionist. It was difficult for Elizabeth to hold such different ideological views from her peers in Richmond. From "the time I knew right from wrong," she later wrote, "it was my sad privilege to differ in many things from the perceived opinions and principles in my locality. This has made my life intensely sad and earnest, and if I may say it tolerant, & uncompromising, but liberal."

After her father's death, shortly before the Civil War began, she and her mother freed the family's slaves. Virginia was already in a state of war—hostility had long been bubbling up between the North and South, most apparently from the time of John Brown's infamous raid at Harpers Ferry in October 1859. Rumors flew about town that the North was getting ready to invade the South, and armed men paced the night expecting troops to come at any moment.

Elizabeth and her mother started caring for wounded and imprisoned Union soldiers in 1861. She persuaded John Winder, Richmond's provost marshal, to let her go on charitable visits to Union prisoners of war. In Richmond, the hotbed capital of the Confederacy, this was risky behavior. Articles appeared in the local papers, including this one in the July 19, 1861, Richmond *Examiner*: "These two women have been expending their opulent means in aiding and giving comfort to the miscreants who have invaded our sacred soil, bent on rapine and murder . . . [and] cannot but be regarded as an evidence of sympathy amounting to an endorsation of the cause and conduct of these Northern Vandals." But Elizabeth brought food and medicine to the convalescing Union troops for a reason: They gave her valuable strategic information to convey to Northern generals. In time she even devised a sophisticated cipher code to carry out missions within the "Richmond Underground," her espionage network. According to the collection of Elizabeth Van Lew Papers at the College of William and Mary, she herself used the code name "Bobsal" to send information. After her death in 1900, the key to her cipher code was found neatly folded in the back of her watchcase.

Elizabeth was nicknamed "Crazy Bet" by her Confederate-sympathizing neighbors—among other things, she walked around mumbling to herself, dressed in shabby clothing—but her "eccentricities" worked well to divert attention from her real activities: bringing clothing, money, and books to Union prisoners held at Richmond's Libby Prison (as well as harboring escapees in her home), sending information across the lines, and buying and freeing slaves. At one point, Mary Bowser, one of the Van Lew's former slaves, worked as a servant for Confederate President Jefferson Davis and his wife in order to learn useful secrets for the "Underground."

Elizabeth periodically wrote in a diary about her activities during the war, but because she was fearful of being found out, she later buried the diary outside her mansion home. The surviving portions of what she called her "occasional journal" were eventually published, along with some of her postwar correspondence. Her words serve to illustrate more clearly the dangers she and her spies braved to ferry information to the Union. "I would if I could give the reader some idea of our daily life during the war," she wrote, "but the keeping of a complete journal was an impossibility and a risk to [sic] fearful to run. Written only to be burnt was the fate of almost everything which would now be of value." Each night when Elizabeth went to bed, she was careful to place next to her anything incriminating that she might have written, "so as to be able to destroy it in a moment."

When Richmond finally fell to Union troops in April 1865, Elizabeth Van Lew was the first to fly the Stars and Stripes over the city once again. To thank her for her services as the Union's "correspondent in Richmond," as Major General Ben Butler called her, General Ulysses Grant visited Elizabeth's home to take tea on her porch. He also appointed her Postmaster General of Richmond for eight years, but that didn't save her from the resentment of her neighbors for a long time afterward. She died in poverty on September 25, 1900. The inscription at her gravesite in Richmond's Shockoe Cemetery reads: "She risked everything that is dear to man—friends, fortune, comfort, health, life itself, all for one absorbing desire of her heart—that slavery might be abolished and the Union preserved."

Any discussion of spies and the freeing of slaves must include Harriet Tubman. The most famous "conductor" of the Underground Railroad, she made repeated trips back to the Confederate states to lead hundreds of slaves north to freedom. Her long life could easily be profiled under any of the chapters in this book—as a soldier, spy, nurse, or rallying figure. Harriet began life as a slave near Cambridge, in Maryland's Dorchester County. Born Araminta Ross to Benjamin Ross and Harriet Green, circa 1821, she later took her mother's name. She worked first as a house servant and then as a field worker when she reached her teenage years.

When she was about twenty-five years old, Harriet married a free black named John Tubman. In 1849 she escaped from the plantation and made her way to Philadelphia, where she found work. During the

A standing portrait of Underground Railroad "conductor" Harriet Tubman.

CREDIT: LIBRARY OF CONGRESS, 3A10453U

1850s she made anywhere from nine to nineteen treacherous trips to bring others—including her parents and her siblings—out of slavery. According to journalist Earl Conrad in his 1943 biography, Harriet said, "I never ran my train off the track and I never lost a passenger," during her time with the Underground Railroad. Deeply religious, she became known as the Moses of her people, and at one time her capture was worth a $40,000 reward.

Once the war began, Harriet Tubman was recruited by the Union army in 1862 to help them on military expeditions on the South Carolina coast, including the June 2, 1863, Combahee River raid in which she helped rescue 756 slaves and secure valuable livestock from the Rebel forces. She also reported on locations of Confederate cotton and ammunition storehouses. In "Narratives of Union Women Spies," Sizer states that Harriet established herself "as a leader in the Combahee River expedition and in undefined spying expeditions." Sizer goes on to say that because her extraordinary abilities and successes were well recognized at the start of the Civil War conflict, Harriet had no need for the "self-promotion" that white spy narratives were created to spin up, and "her services were requested by a government well aware" of her work.

In Sarah H. Bradford's 1869 biography, *Scenes in the Life of Harriet Tubman*, the author described Harriet as a "fearless woman," one who was often sent out into Confederate territory as a spy and who "brought back valuable information as to the position of armies and batteries; she has been in battle when the shot was falling like hail . . . but the thought of fear never seems to have had place for a moment in her mind." In her espionage work, Bradford noted, Harriet was instrumental in getting slaves to trust the Union soldiers: "It became quite important that she should accompany expeditions . . . into unexplored parts of the country, to control and get information from those whom they took with them as guides."

In addition to her work as a scout and spy under Colonel James Montgomery for the Second South Carolina Volunteers, Harriet nursed the sick and wounded in Florida and the Carolinas. After the war she continued tirelessly to help freedmen by raising money and getting clothing for the poor. In 1896 she made an inspiring appearance at the organizing meeting of the National Association of Colored Women in Washington, D.C. She settled in Auburn, New York, and worked to open a home for the aged and indigent in 1908. Although it enlisted Harriet's help and used her vast knowledge of the Southern states during the Civil War, the U.S. government refused to grant her a military pension based on her own merits until thirty years later, in 1899. She died on March 10, 1913. Her tombstone reads simply, "Servant of God, Well Done."

Wartime Nurses

CLARA BARTON, CORNELIA HANCOCK,

MARY LIVERMORE, MARY ANNE BICKERDYKE,

BELLE REYNOLDS, SALLY TOMPKINS, AND KATE CUMMING

"Like a ministering angel, [she] attended to the wants of as many of the wounded and dying soldiers as she could, thus winning the gratitude and esteem of the brave fellows by whom she was surrounded."

—description of Major Belle Reynolds,
Peoria Daily Transcript, *April 22, 1862*

IN SEPTEMBER 1862 CLARA BARTON was working tirelessly as a nurse and aid worker during the battle of Antietam when a bullet pierced the sleeve of her dress and killed the man she was caring for. She saw the battlefield at its worst, and, after six weeks of ministering to the wounded, she contracted typhoid fever. What Clara encountered was par for the course for wartime nurses in the field. These women braved many of the dangers that male soldiers did—they were present on the battlefield, skirting artillery fire as they attempted to care for the injured. Although most

Civil War nurses spent the bulk of their time working in fixed army hospitals, all combated other enemies such as disease and a profound lack of resources, both human and material. Not yet welcome or respected within the male sphere of medicine, they all fought prejudice against their gender and their profession. Many Northerners and Southerners perceived women who worked as nurses—through their work privy to seeing men in their most intimate and vulnerable states— as little better than prostitutes.

After the First Battle of Bull Run in July 1861, Clara Barton was one of the nurses who tended to the Union wounded as they arrived in Washington, D.C. Supplies poured in after she placed an ad in a Massachusetts newspaper, and she established a distribution agency to allocate the goods. From this she started to see the potential for setting up a wartime relief agency to provide for the troops. The experience was only the beginning of a long and accomplished life spent breaking new ground in relief organization.

In August 1862 Clara secured official permission to bring food and medicine directly to regiments on the field in Virginia and Maryland. That month she spent two days nursing those injured in the battle of Cedar Mountain, Virginia. Humanitarian to the core, she was nonpartisan in her treatment of the wounded and dying, helping both Union and Confederate soldiers during that and other conflicts. In the following years, she traveled with the Army of the Potomac for a time and brought hospital wagons to care for the wounded. She worked during the most intense military engagements. In addition to Antietam, she saw the carnage following the May 1864 Wilderness Campaign, during which she kept valuable notes on the discouraging state of medical

A photograph of nursing pioneer Clara Barton.
CREDIT: NATIONAL ARCHIVES PHOTO NO. 111-B-1857

care at Fredericksburg, where she was tending to those who were moved from the front: "I saw them [the soldiers] lying there early this morning—they had been wounded two and three days previous . . . and after all this lay still another night without care or food or shelter, many doubtless famished after arriving in Fredericksburg." Clara was also present at the sieges of Petersburg and Richmond, close to the end of the war, and was dubbed the "angel of the battlefield" by the grateful soldiers for whom she cared.

Even in postbellum peacetime, Clara continued to be a pioneer in the organization of charitable aid and relief societies, eventually touring extensively on the lecture circuit. Just prior to his assassination, President Abraham Lincoln gave her permission to embark on a search for missing soldiers and help reunite survivors with their relatives. In February 1865 Clara worked with the War Department to set up the Missing Soldiers Office. According to the Library of Congress, she researched and tracked down information about 22,000 soldiers during the following three years. She also supervised the grave-marking of more than 13,000 anonymously buried soldiers at Georgia's infamous Andersonville prison, founding the first national cemetery. Perhaps her most notable accomplishment was spearheading the movement to found the American Red Cross. She was elected as the first president of the organization on June 29, 1881, in Washington, D.C.

Her poem "The Women Who Went to the Field" (reprinted at the end of this chapter) effectively evoked the idea of smashing stereotypes—a feat that she and many other women accomplished as they took to the hospitals and front lines as aid workers. Indeed, this poem called attention to some of the most prominent names in wartime nursing: Mary Ann Bickerdyke, Cornelia Hancock, Dorothea Dix, Mary Livermore, and Annie Etheridge. Clara Barton was careful to note that these were but a handful of the women who performed admirably as nurses during the Civil War period, much beloved by the soldiers and officers who witnessed their unflagging efforts. Proving themselves in this capacity, Civil War nurses helped shift attitudes about women and their abilities away from the traditional fallacy that they would "just be in the way" to the indisputable fact that they'd become—in Clara Barton's words—"nurses, consolers, and saviours of men."

Wartime nurses weren't only saviors of men, however. While at Antietam, Clara Barton was nursing a soldier for a chest wound when, to her surprise, she discovered that her patient was actually a woman named Mary Galloway. Female soldiers in disguise and nurses working openly as women were breaking new ground alongside one another during the war. Anecdotal evidence suggests that female nurses were particularly attuned to recognizing members of their sex in disguise as soldiers. In her memoir of the war, Mary Livermore detailed her realization during a drilling exercise that one soldier of the Nineteenth Illinois was really a woman. Many of these soldiers were actually discovered only when they were ill or wounded, requiring medical attention, or when they were killed in battle. In her article "Women Soldiers of the Civil War," DeAnne Blanton cites a February 10, 1901, New York *Sun* article that mentioned Mary Owens, who was discovered as a woman after she was wounded in the arm—she had served for eighteen months as "John Evans." Blanton also notes the example of Mary Scaberry of Columbus, Ohio, aka Charles Freeman, a private in the Fifty-second Ohio Infantry. After serving for sixteen weeks, she was admitted to a general hospital in Louisville, Kentucky, on November 10, 1862, for a high fever and was eventually discharged from service on the grounds of what army personnel called "Sextual incompatibility." In letters that some incredulous soldiers sent home, there are anecdotes of female soldiers who remained undetected until they gave birth—some even during picket duty, or in the thick of battle.

Official U.S. War Department records document the discovery of a female soldier's body dressed as a Confederate private at Gettysburg, on July 17, 1863. Also present on the battlefield during this time was a fresh-faced twenty-three-year-old New Jersey native named Cornelia Hancock. "We have been two days on the field; go out about eight and come in about six—go in ambulances or army buggies . . . I feel assured I shall never feel horrified at anything that may happen to me hereafter," she wrote to her sister on July 8, 1863. She volunteered to be a nurse when her brother-in-law, an army doctor, asked her to help relieve and care for the wounded.

Cornelia was overwhelmed by the lack of surgeons and supplies. Hundreds of injured soldiers, their wounds not yet dressed, had to wait long periods for the medical attentions of few staff. Many of those hurt had no clothing, sheets, or tents to lie under, and the nurses canvased desperately for wool blankets and other provisions from local homes. "The citizens are stripped of everything they have," she wrote from Gettysburg, noting that for everyone involved it was an "exhausting state of affairs."

Because of this chronic lack of supplies—"I would like to see seven barrels of dried rusk [sweetened bread] here," Cornelia wrote longingly to her sister—Civil War nurses were ingenious in their treatment of various ailments, often coming up with substitute materials and home remedies. In her book *From Hardtack to Home Fries: An Uncommon History of American Cooks and Meals,* food historian Barbara Haber describes the wartime strategy of feeding soldiers who suffered from chronic diarrhea a diet of roast beef, radishes, and cabbage to alleviate their symptoms.

Various volunteer organizations offered support in the relief efforts, but the one that really made the difference was the United States Sanitary Commission. "If it were not for the Sanitary, much suffering would ensue," wrote Cornelia. The U.S. Sanitary Commission was approved in 1861 by President Lincoln to help get food, clothing, medical care, and aid supplies to the North's soldiers during the war. Although doctors and inspectors were men, the local chapters were almost exclusively made up of and headed by women. All the services provided were subsidized by donations and "Sanitary Fair" fund-raisers. One of the Sanitary Commission's founders was Elizabeth Blackwell, the first American woman to receive a degree in medicine. With its main headquarters in Washington, D.C., and ten regional offices throughout the North, the Sanitary Commission contributed about $20 million to the Union war effort by the end of the war, along with countless hours of volunteer labor. Two key organizers with the Sanitary Commission were Mary Livermore and Mary Ann Bickerdyke.

Born in Boston in 1820, Mary Livermore was forty years old when the Civil War began and had worked as a teacher for many years. Her husband was a Universalist minister, and the sect's concept of inclusive salvation appealed to her sense of social activism (mostly in the antislavery and temperance movements). Mary's work prior to the war groomed her for her role during the conflict. She saw the need for food, clothing, and other relief efforts and joined the Chicago (which later became the Northwestern) chapter of the U.S. Sanitary Commission. She would later become co-director of the Chicago office along with fellow soldier's aid advocate Jane Hoge.

She documented her influential time with the Sanitary Commission in her 1887 autobiography, *My Story of the War*. Like most nurses, she cared for the wounded and dying, but one of her biggest successes was a three-state hospital inspection tour with Jane Hoge in southern Illinois, Kentucky, and Missouri. The two women surveyed filthy camp and hospital conditions and drastic food shortages and, after the tour, organized and shipped 80,000 packages of food and supplies—worth a total of $1 million—to those hospitals and battlefields that needed them most. Their speaking engagements also helped inspire others to develop local aid societies. At war's end, Mary Livermore turned her considerable abilities toward the women's suffrage movement and was elected as the first president of the Association for Advancement of Women and president of the American Woman Suffrage Association.

Mary Ann Bickerdyke was one of the first women to attend and graduate from Oberlin College in Ohio. She later studied nursing and was one of the war's early volunteers at a field hospital in Cairo, Illinois, in June 1861. There she much improved conditions at the substandard facility, becoming matron of the hospital in just five months. A field agent for the Northwestern branch of the Sanitary Commission, Mary was nicknamed "Mother" Bickerdyke for her caring and gentle manner. She was also known for her resourcefulness—the ability to forage for and prepare nutritious meals and keep wounds and sheets clean in the absence of sufficient food and supplies. Her talents gained her the admiration of General Ulysses Grant, who gave her a pass to travel with his army and aid the wounded. In summer 1864 she joined General William T. Sherman's march through Georgia on his way to capture Atlanta. His orders from Grant in this decisive cam-

Union nurse Mary Ann "Mother" Bickerdyke, in profile.
CREDIT: LIBRARY OF CONGRESS, LC-USZ62-79788

paign were to inflict "all the damage you can against their [the enemy's] war resources." In place of the destruction wreaked by Sherman and his army, however, Mary Ann Bickerdyke created a series of hospitals in her wake and made sure soldiers received proper medical examinations.

Without the benefit of the U.S. Sanitary Commission behind them, Confederate nurses set up hundreds of local relief societies to get necessary provisions to their own army. During the war, the Confederacy had roughly one-quarter the number of surgeons and assistant surgeons as the Union army's Medical Department. Union blockades also further limited the medical supplies the South could acquire, and many Southern women smuggled contraband drugs in such places as their hoop skirts. Even more than their Northern counterparts, Confederate doctors and nurses had to rely on alternative remedies. According to the Library of Congress, the South's Surgeon General Samuel P. Moore "encouraged doctors to substitute native plants as medicines," and Dr. Francis P. Porcher's widely read 1863 book, *Resources of Southern Fields and Forests, Medical, Economical, and Agricultural,* advised such cures as horehound juice for colds.

Perhaps the most famous Confederate nurse was Sally Tompkins, who turned a private home in Richmond, Virginia, into the Robertson Hospital, one of the South's biggest wartime hospitals. The everyday workings of the hospital depended on female nurses, including slaves. By the end of the war, she had treated a vast number of patients— 1,333 wounded and sick soldiers—and was able to save all but 73 of them. When private hospitals were closed in the Southern states, President Jefferson Davis granted her the rank of Confederate captain so that she could continue to operate her infirmary.

But most Southern women faced at least some resentment and resistance in hospitals throughout the war, even as they were recruited to join the war effort. In her memoir, *A Southern Woman's Story,* Phoebe Pember reported the widespread hostility she encountered

among male doctors when she became a matron at Richmond's
Chimborazo Hospital. The rigid sexual boundaries of Southern society were difficult to transcend. In his essay "'Missing in Action':
Women of the Confederacy," George Rable explores the ways in
which Southern women toed the line between breaking social custom
and reinforcing the gender hierarchy. The necessities of war extended
the traditional female role of tending to the home front. In addition
to sewing flags and uniforms, women began running businesses and
plantations while husbands took to the battlefield. Nursing became the
center of the gender debate and exemplified "the complexity of . . .
wartime attitudes toward change," states Drew Faust in "Altars of
Sacrifice: Confederate Women and the Narratives of War." Even those
advocates of women entering the medical sphere emphasized that they
should be "auxiliaries" and not try to "direct or control the physician."

"I could fill whole pages with descriptions of the scenes before me,"
wrote Kate Cumming, who in April 1862 defied her family to volunteer as a nurse in a Confederate hospital in Corinth, Alabama. The
experiences she detailed made it clear that female nurses were vital in
caring for the thousands of soldiers who emerged from the bloodshed
of battle. She described the devotion of nurses who had "special
patients, whom they never leave. One of them, from Natchez, Miss.,
has been constantly by a young man, badly wounded, ever since she
came here, and the doctors say that she has been the means of saving
his life. Many of the others are doing the same." It's possible that the
chance to make a difference—outside the confines of the home—made
these nurses even more effective and dedicated to their jobs: "I have not
even time to speak to them [Mrs. Ogden and the other Mobile ladies]

. . . I have been busy all day, and can scarcely tell what I have been doing; I have not taken time to even eat, and certainly not time to sit down." Even Northern nurses such as Cornelia Hancock felt that despite the frantic pace and the suffering they witnessed, "there is all in getting to do what you *want* to do and I am doing that."

In an April 12 diary entry, Kate Cumming noted that the doctors at the hospital complained "very much at the manner in which" certain men were rotated every few hours in and out of the facility for nurse duty. "I can not see how it is possible for them to take proper care of the men, as nursing is a thing that has to be learned, and we should select our best men for it—as I am certain that none but good, conscientious persons will ever do justice to the patients." She eventually took charge of food and housekeeping departments in several Georgia hospitals, and her diary was later published in 1866 as *A Journal of Hospital Life in the Confederate Army of Tennessee.*

Though the idea of female nurses eventually gained wider societal approval on both sides of the conflict, the notion of female doctors was still radically extreme. Dr. Mary Edwards Walker was one of a handful of women physicians who graduated from Syracuse Medical College in 1855. After serving as a nurse during various engagements, including the First Battle of Bull Run and Chickamauga, she went on to become the first female surgeon in the Union army's medical services. While tending to the wounded, Dr. Walker wore men's clothing to more easily respond to the demands of her job on the front and in field hospitals. As commissioned assistant surgeon for the Fifty-second Ohio Infantry, she also reportedly served as a spy for the Union.

Dr. Mary Walker was captured by Confederate forces in April 1864 and held as a prisoner of war in Richmond for four months. She treated civilians on both sides of the battle lines and also gave medical care to other prisoners. For her heroism and Civil War service, she was awarded the Congressional Medal of Honor in 1866, the first and only woman to have received it. The medal was revoked in 1917 but reinstated posthumously by Congress in 1977.

The Civil War signaled a definitive transition in the popular view of women in the medical services, who came to be depicted as heroines during the course of their work. Belle Reynolds came to local prominence when she joined her husband, Lieutenant William S. Reynolds, in the ranks of the Seventeenth Illinois Infantry. She was renowned for her attentive nursing and "meritorious conduct" at the Battle of Shiloh (aka Pittsburg Landing, Tennessee). To reward her work, Governor Richard Yates of Illinois gave her a formal commission as a major, which the Peoria *Daily Transcript* called an "unprecedented military appointment" on April 22, 1862. She was commended for sharing with her husband the "dangers and privations of a soldier's life," and the newspaper noted that it was probable that "no lady in America will ever again have such a distinguished military honor conferred upon her." Belle was similarly lauded in *Harper's Weekly* on May 17, 1862, where her portrait was published. The *Harper's* piece made much of Belle's attachment to one of the most active regiments in the war and of the fact that she did not receive any special treatment as a woman when she traveled along with the army. She shared "a soldier's fare" in camp, slept "upon the ground in the open air, with no covering other than her

A portrait of Illinois nurse Belle Reynolds.
CREDIT: FROM *WOMEN OF THE WAR* (1866)

blanket, and frequently drenched with rain," and completed long marches in the middle of the night alongside the best male soldiers in the regiment. Highly regarded by the army members she cared for, Belle was similarly celebrated by the citizens of Peoria; they sent a letter of

approval to Governor Yates after her appointment as major. But even as
lauded as she was for her nursing work, there were still some who
begrudged her achievements. An article in the May 22, 1862, Peoria
Daily Transcript hinted at "domestic trouble" with her husband that may
have come as a result of Belle's appointment.

Other notable nurses who worked during the Civil War included
Dorothea Dix, a social reformer for the mentally ill who volunteered to
become Union superintendent of female nurses in 1861. She started
the Federal army nursing program, in which more than 3,000 women
would eventually serve, and called for a strict dress code and regulations, leading to markedly improved medical care under her jurisdic-
tion. Ella King Newsom, nicknamed the "Florence Nightingale of the
South," supervised operations for Tennessee hospitals at Memphis
and Nashville and worked as the matron of Chattanooga's Academy
Hospital. And Susie King Taylor, an escaped slave who became a
nurse for the Thirty-third U.S. Colored Troops, wrote *Reminiscences of
my life in camp with the 33d United States Colored Troops, late 1st S.C.
Volunteers*, a 1902 book about her work during the war. With the
encouragement of the regiment's commanding officer, Colonel C. T.
Trowbridge, she wrote one of the only accounts of a black woman's
wartime experiences.

Clara Barton's poem, printed below, is effectively a tribute not only
to women nurses but to all women who bravely "went to the field" to
serve as soldiers, spies, daughters of the regiment, or caregivers, working vigorously and beyond the call of duty for their respective causes
during the American Civil War.

The Women Who Went to the Field

By Clara Barton

The women who went to the field, you say,

The women who went to the field; and pray,

What did they go for?—just to be in the way?—

They'd not know the difference betwixt work and play,

What did they know about war, anyway ?

What could they do?—of what use could they be?

They would scream at the sight of a gun, don't you see?

Just fancy them round where the bugle notes play,

And the long roll is bidding us on to the fray.

Imagine their skirts 'mong artillery wheels,

And watch for their flutter as they flee 'cross the fields

When the charge is rammed home and the fire belches hot;—

They never will wait for the answering shot.

They would faint at the first drop of blood, in their sight.

What fun for us boys,—(ere we enter the fight;)

They might pick some lint, and tear up some sheets,

And make us some jellies, and send on their sweets,

And knit some soft socks for Uncle Sam's shoes,

And write us some letters, and tell us the news.

And thus it was settled by common consent,

That husbands, or brothers, or whoever went,

That the place for the women was in their own homes,

There to patiently wait until victory comes.

But later, it chanced, just how no one knew,
That the lines slipped a bit, and some 'gan to crowd through;
And they went,—where did they go?—Ah; where did they not?
Show us the battle,—the field,—or the spot
Where the groans of the wounded rang out on the air
That her ear caught it not, and her hand was not there,
Who wiped the death sweat from the cold, clammy brow,
And sent home the message;—" 'T is well with him now"?
Who watched in the tents, whilst the fever fires burned,
And the pain-tossing limbs in agony turned,
And wet the parched tongue, calmed delirium's strife
Till the dying lips murmured, " My Mother," " My Wife"!
And who were they all ?—They were many, my men:
Their record was kept by no tabular pen:
They exist in traditions from father to son.
Who recalls, in dim memory, now here and there one.—
A few names where writ, and by chance live to-day;
But's a perishing record fast fading away.
Of those we recall, there are scarcely a score,
Dix, Dame, Bickerdyke,—Edson, Harvey and Moore,
Fales, Wittenmeyer, Gilson, Safford and Lee,
And poor Cutter dead in the sands of the sea;
And Frances D. Gage, our "Aunt Fanny" of old,
Whose voice rang for freedom when freedom was sold.
And Husband, and Etheridge, and Harlan and Case,
Livermore, Alcott, Hancock and Chase,

And Turner, and Hawley, and Potter and Hall,
Ah! the list grows apace, as they come at the call:
Did these women quail at the sight of a gun?
Will some soldier tell us of one he saw run?
Will he glance at the boats on the great western flood,
At Pittsburg and Shiloh, did they faint at the blood?
And the brave wife of Grant stood there with them then,
And her calm, stately presence gave strength to his men.
And Marie of Logan; she went with them too;
A bride, scarcely more than a sweetheart, 't is true.
Her young cheek grows pale when the bold troopers ride.
Where the "Black Eagle" soars, she is close at his side,
She staunches his blood, cools the fever-burnt breath,
And the wave of her hand stays the Angel of Death;
She nurses him back, and restores once again
To both army and state the brave leader of men.
She has smoothed his black plumes and laid them to sleep,
Whilst the angels above them their high vigils keep:
And she sits here alone, with the snow on her brow—
Your cheers for her comrades! Three cheers for her now.
And these were the women who went to the war:
The women of question; what did they go for?
Because in their hearts God had planted the seed
Of pity for woe, and help for its need;
They saw, in high purpose, a duty to do,
And the armor of right broke the barriers through.

Uninvited, unaided, unsanctioned ofttimes,

With pass, or without it, they pressed on the lines;

They pressed, they implored, till they ran the lines through,

And this was the "running" the men saw them do.

'T was a hampered work, its worth largely lost;

'T was hindrance, and pain, and effort, and cost:

But through these came knowledge,—knowledge is power.—

And never again in the deadliest hour

Of war or of peace shall we be so beset

To accomplish the purpose our spirits have met.

And what would they do if war came again?

The scarlet cross floats where all was blank then.

They would bind on their "brassards" and march to the fray,

And the man liveth not who could say to them nay;

They would stand with you now, as they stood with you then,

The nurses, consolers, and saviours of men.

Bibliography

The Abraham Lincoln Papers at the Library of Congress. Series 1, General Correspondence, 1833–1916. A letter from Belle Boyd Hardinge to Abraham Lincoln, January 24, 1865. Available on-line at memory.loc.gov.

American Antiquarian Society. Available on-line at www.american antiquarian.org.

American Battlefield Protection Program, National Park Service. Available on-line at www2.cr.nps.gov/abpp/index.htm.

American Museum of Photography. Available on-line at www. photographymuseum.com.

Bernstein, Iver. *The New York City Draft Riots: Their Significance for American Society and Politics in the Age of Civil War.* New York: Oxford University Press, 1990.

Blanton, DeAnne. "Women Soldiers of the Civil War." *Prologue: Quarterly of the National Archives* (spring 1993). Available on-line at www.nara.gov.

Blanton, DeAnne, and Lauren M. Cook. *They Fought Like Demons: Women Soldiers in the American Civil War.* Baton Rouge: Louisiana State University Press, 2002.

Boyd, Belle. *Belle Boyd in Camp and Prison.* Documenting the American South: University of North Carolina at Chapel Hill Libraries. Available on-line at docsouth.unc.edu/boyd/menu.html.

Bradford, Sarah Hopkins. *Scenes in the Life of Harriet Tubman.* Auburn: W. J. Moses, 1869. Documenting the American South: University of North Carolina at Chapel Hill Libraries. Available on-line at docsouth.unc.edu/neh/bradford/menu.html.

Bullough, Vern L., Olga Maranjian Church, and Alice P. Stein. *American Nursing: A Biographical Dictionary.* New York, London: Garland Publishing, Inc., 1988.

Burgess, Lauren Cook, ed. *An Uncommon Soldier: The Civil War Letters of Sarah Rosetta Wakeman, alias Pvt. Lyons Wakeman, 153rd Regiment, New York State Volunteers, 1862–1864.* New York: Oxford University Press, 1994.

Chesebro Genealogy. Available on-line at www.chesebro.net.

The Civil War: A film by Ken Burns, prod. and dir. Ken Burns, 690 mins., PBS Home Video, 1990, videocassette and DVD. Additional information available on-line at www.pbs.org/civilwar.

"Civil War Nurse Clara Barton's Memorabilia Found," *NurseWeek Magazine* (15 December, 1997). Available on-line at www.nurse week.com.

Clara Barton National Historic Site. Available on-line at www.nps.gov/clba.

Clausius, Gerhard. "The Little Soldier of the Ninety-fifth: Albert D. J. Cashier." *Journal of the Illinois State Historical Society,* (1958). Available on-line at www.alliancelibrarysystem.org.

Clinton, Catherine. *The Other Civil War: American Women in the Nineteenth Century.* New York: Farrar, Strauss, & Giroux, 1999.

Clinton, Catherine, and Nina Silber, eds. *Divided Houses: Gender and the Civil War.* New York: Oxford University Press, 1992.

Coco, Gregory A. *The Civil War Infantryman: In Camp, on the March, and in Battle.* Gettysburg: Thomas Publications, 1996.

Confederate States of America Surgeon-General's Office Standard Supply Table of the Indigenous Remedies for Field Service and the Sick in General Hospitals. [Richmond?]: s.n., 1863. Documenting the American South, University of North Carolina at Chapel Hill Libraries. Available on-line at docsouth.unc.edu/imls/remedies/menu.html.

Conklin, Mike. "Jennie Came Marching Home: Downstate Women Battle to Preserve the Memory of a Civil War Soldier Who Spent Most of Her Life Posing as a Man," *Chicago Tribune,* 5 September, 2001.

Cumming, Kate. *A Journal of Hospital Life in the Confederate Army of Tennessee.* Louisville: John P. Morgan & Co.; New Orleans: W. Evelyn, 1866.

Dannett, Sylvia G. L. *She Rode with the Generals: The True and Incredible Story of Sarah Emma Seelye, alias Franklin Thompson*. New York: T. Nelson, 1960.

Dyer, Frederick H. *Dyer's Compendium of the War of the Rebellion*. Des Moines: The Dyer Publishing Company, 1908. Available on-line at U.S. Army Military Institute, carlisle–www.army.mil/usamhi.

Earl Conrad/Harriet Tubman Collection, 1939–1941 (1946). New York Public Library Digital Collections. Available on-line at digilib.nypl.org.

Edmonds, Sarah Emma. *Memoirs of a Soldier, Nurse and Spy*. DeKalb: Northern Illinois University Press, 1999.

Edmonds, S. Emma. *Nurse and Spy in the Union Army: Comprising the Adventures and Experiences of a Woman in Hospitals, Camps, and Battle-Fields*. Hartford: W. S. Williams & Co., 1865.

Elizabeth Van Lew Papers, Manuscripts and Rare Books Department, Swem Library, College of William and Mary. Available on-line at www.swem.wm.edu.

Encyclopaedia Britannica. Available on-line at www.eb.com.

Farquhar, Michael. " 'Rebel Rose,' A Spy of Grande Dame Proportions." *The Washington Post*, 18 September, 2000, p. A01. Available on-line at www.washingtonpost.com.

Faust, Drew. "Altars of Sacrifice: Confederate Women and the Narratives of War," *Journal of American History* 76 (March 1990).

Faust, Drew. *Mothers of Invention: Women of the Slaveholding South in the American Civil War.* New York: Vintage Books, 1997.

Faust, Patricia L., ed. *The Illustrated Encyclopedia of the Civil War.* New York: Harper & Row, 1986.

Fox, William F. *Regimental Losses in the American Civil War 1861–1865.* Dayton: Morningside Bookshop, 1985.

Gienapp, William E. "Abraham Lincoln and the Border States." *Journal of the Abraham Lincoln Association* 13 (1992).

Gorman, Michael D. Civil War Richmond: An on-line research project designed to collect documents, photographs, and maps pertaining to Richmond, Virginia, during the Civil War. Available on-line at www.mdgorman.com.

Greenhow, Rose O'Neal. *My Imprisonment and the First Year of Abolition Rule at Washington, 1814–1864.* Documenting the American South: University of North Carolina at Chapel Hill Libraries. Available on-line at docsouth.unc.edu/greenhow/menu.html.

Hall, Richard. *Patriots in Disguise.* New York: Paragon House, 1993.

Hancock, Cornelia. "A Union Nurse at Gettysburg." *South After Gettysburg: Letters of Cornelia Hancock from the Army of the Potomac, 1863–1865.* Philadelphia: University of Pennsylvania Press, 1937.

Historical Collections from the Library of Congress's National Digital Library. Available on-line at memory.loc.gov.

History of the 17th Illinois Infantry. Report of the Adjutant General of the State of Illinois (Vol. 2, 1861–1866, 1900, p. 61). Illinois Alive! Alliance Library System. Available on-line at www.alliancelibrarysystem.com.

Hughes, Susan Lyons. "The Daughter of the Regiment: A Brief History of Vivandières and Cantinières in the American Civil War." Available on-line at www.ehistory.com/uscw/features/articles/0005/vivandieres.cfm.

Lambert, Craig. "Rifles and Typhus: The Deadliest War" (including interview with Drew Gilpin Faust), *Harvard Magazine* 103, no. 5 (May–June 2001): 15.

Leonard, Elizabeth D. *All the Daring of the Soldier: Women of the Civil War Armies*. New York: W. W. Norton & Company, Inc., 1999.

LeVert, Suzanne. *The Civil War Society's Encyclopedia of the Civil War*. New York: The Random House, 1997.

Livermore, Mary. *My Story of the War: A Woman's Narrative of Four Years Personal Experience*. Hartford: A. D. Worthington, 1887.

Livermore, Thomas. *Numbers and Losses in the Civil War in America 1861–5*. Boston and New York: Houghton, Mifflin and Company, 1901.

Lunt, Dolly. *A Woman's Wartime Journal*. New York: The Century Company, 1918.

McPherson, James. *What They Fought For: 1861–1865*. New York: Anchor Books, 1994.

McPherson, James M. *The Atlas of the Civil War*. New York: Macmillan Publishing Co., 1994.

Moore, Frank. *Women of the War; Their Heroism and Self–Sacrifice*. Hartford: S.S. Scranton & Co., 1866. Available on-line at www.hti.umich.edu.

"Mrs. Major Reynolds." *Harper's Weekly*, (17 May, 1862): 306. Illinois Alive! Alliance Library System. Available on-line at www.alliance librarysystem.com.

National Archives and Records Administration, Old Military and Civil Records Division of the National Archives. Available on-line at www.nara.gov.

National Museum of Civil War Medicine. Available on-line at www.civilwarmed.org.

National Park Service. Available on-line at www.nps.gov.

National Portrait Gallery, Smithsonian Institution. Mathew Brady Gallery. Available on-line at www.npg.si.edu.

Official records of the Union and Confederate Armies. *The War of the Rebellion: A Compilation of the Official Records of the Union and Confederate Armies*. The Making of America Project, Cornell University. Available on-line at library5.library.cornell.edu/moa/ moa_browse.html.

Pember, Phoebe Yates. *A Southern Woman's Story*. New York: G. W. Carleton and Company, 1879.

Pryor, Elizabeth Brown. *Clara Barton: Professional Angel*. Philadelphia: University of Pennsylvania Press, 1987.

Rable, George. " 'Missing in Action': Women of the Confederacy," in *Divided Houses: Gender and the Civil War*. Edited by Catherine Clinton and Nina Silber. New York: Oxford University Press, 1992.

Richardson, Albert D. *The Secret Service, the Field, the Dungeon, and the Escape*. Hartford: American Publishing, 1865.

"A Romantic Story of a Female Soldier." *Chelsea Telegraph and Pioneer* 4 June, 1864, 3.

Rose O'Neal Greenhow Papers. Special Collections, Duke University. Available on-line at scriptorium.lib.duke.edu/collections/civil-war-women.html.

Ryan, David D. *A Yankee Spy in Richmond: The Civil War Diary of 'Crazy Bet' Van Lew*. Mechanicsburg: Stackpole Books, 1996.

Sartin, Jeffrey S. "Infectious Diseases During the Civil War: The Triumph of the 'Third Army.' " *Clinical Infectious Diseases* 16 (1993):580–4. Available on-line at www.imsdocs.com/civilwar.htm.

"Shall We Have a Federal Union?" *New York Tribune*, 27 February, 1861.

Sifakis, Stewart. *Who Was Who in the Civil War*. New York: Facts on File, 1988.

Sizer, Lyde Cullen. "Acting Her Part: Narratives of Union Women Spies," in *Divided Houses: Gender and the Civil War*. Edited by Catherine Clinton and Nina Silber. New York: Oxford University Press, 1992.

Sizer, Lyde Cullen. "Loreta Janeta Velazquez," in *American National Biography*. Oxford University Press, 1999. American Council of Learned Societies. Available on-line at www.libarts.ucok.edu.

Smith, David V. M. "The Hardships of Soldiering." A soldier's letter from the Gilder Lehrman Institute of American History (1862).

The Smithsonian Institution. "Civil War Leaders: Rose O'Neal Greenhow." Available on-line at www.civilwar.si.edu/leaders_green how.html.

Spalding, Peg. "Union Maid." Illinois Alive! McLean County Historical Society, Alliance Library System. Available on-line at www.alliancelibrarysystem.com.

Spies, Scouts, and Raiders. Alexandria, Va.: Time–Life Books, 1983.

Stampp, Kenneth. "The Southern Road to Appomattox: The Problem of Morale in the Confederacy." *Cotton Memorial Papers*, no. 4: 246–269. Texas Western Press, 1969.

Stone, Sarah Katherine. *Brokenburn: The Journal of Kate Stone, 1861–1868*. Edited by John Q. Anderson. Baton Rouge: Louisiana State University Press, 1995.

"Tale of Two Identities: Woman Who Fought in Civil War as Man Stayed at Vets Home," *The Quincy-Herald Whig*. 19 June, 1995. Available on-line at www.alliancelibrarysystem.com.

Taylor, Susie King. *Reminiscences of My Life in Camp with the 33d United States Colored Troops Late 1st S.C. Volunteers*. Boston: Published by the author, 1902. New York Public Library Digital Edition available on-line at www.digilib.npl.org.

The Time of the Lincolns. (Companion web site to Abraham and Mary Lincoln: *A House Divided*.) In PBS [web site], 2001, A David Grubin Productions, Inc.; available on-line at www.pbs.org/wgbh/amex/lincolns.

Tompkins-McCaw Library for the Health Sciences, Virginia Commonwealth University. Available on-line at www.library.vcu.edu/tml/bibs/cwmed.html.

Tortorello, Michael. "Babes in Armies," *City Pages* 17, no. 798 (20 March, 1996). Available on-line at www.citypages.com/data bank/17/798/article2594.asp.

United States Army Military History Institute. Available on-line at carlisle–www.army.mil/usamhi.

United States Sanitary Commission Records, 1861–1872. Manuscripts and Archives Division, The New York Public Library. Available on-line at www.nypl.org.

"An Unprecedented Military Appointment," *Peoria Daily Transcript*, 22 April, 1862. Illinois Alive! Alliance Library System. Available on-line at www.alliancelibrarysystem.com.

Velazquez, Loreta Janeta. *The Woman in Battle: A Narrative of the Exploits, Adventures, and Travels of Madame Loreta Janeta Velazquez, Otherwise Known as Lieutenant Harry T. Buford, Confederate States Army*. Richmond: Dustin, Gilman & Co., 1876.

"Votes for Women: Selections from the National American Woman Suffrage Association Collection, 1848–1921." Rare Book and Special Collections Division, Library of Congress. Available on-line at www.memory.loc.gov/ammem/naw/nawshome.html.

Wagner, Margaret E., Gary W. Gallagher, Paul Finkelman, eds. *The Library of Congress Civil War Desk Reference*. New York: Simon & Schuster, 2002.

"Wanted—A Policy!" *The New York Times*, 3 April, 1861.

The White House. Available on-line at www.whitehouse.gov.

Wiley, Bell Irvin. *The Life of Billy Yank: The Common Soldier of the Union*. Baton Rouge: Louisiana State University Press, 1952.

"Woman Who Masqueraded as Man," *The Quincy (Ill.) Whig,* c. 1914. Courtesy of the Illinois Veterans Home. Illinois Alive! Alliance Library System. Available on-line at www.alliance librarysystem.com.

Women and the Civil War: Manuscript sources in the Special Collections Library at Duke University. Available on-line at scriptorium.lib.duke.edu/women/civilwar.html.

Women and War: An Exhibit of Photographs from the Schlesinger Library. Radcliffe Institute for Advanced Study, Harvard University. Available on-line at www.radcliffe.edu.

"The Yankee Despotism in Washington." *Richmond Whig* 16 April, 1861.

Index

A

All the Daring of the Soldier, 31–32, 41, 48, 56, 60, 71, 73

American Association for the Advancement of Women, 116

American National Biography, 31

American Red Cross, 112

American Revolutionary War, 1, 7, 76

American Woman Suffrage Association, 116

Anable, Harvey, 37

Andrews, J.E., 61

Antietam, battle of, 13, 82, 109–10, 113

Appomattox Court House, 85

Aquitaine, Eleanor of, 1

Arc, Joan of, 1, 24, 33, 97

Austin, William Henry, 47

B

Baker, Hilary, 100

Baker, J.H., 71

Ball's Bluff, battle of, 30

Banks, Nathaniel P., 49

Barnum, P.T., 100

Barton, Clara, 5, 109–13, 123, 124–27

Battles
  Antietam, 13, 82, 109–10, 113
  Ball's Bluff, 30
  Bull Run, 14, 28, 30, 78, 81, 88–89, 110, 120
  Chancellorsville, 83
  Chantilly, 83
  Fort Donelson, 30
  Fort Sumter, 9, 74
  Fredericksburg, 74, 82, 83, 111
  Gettysburg, 82, 114
  Red River, 56
  Richmond, 70